¡Jon le Bon!

Based on an original idea by Alex A.

First published in French in 2013 by Presses Aventure under the title *Le frigo temporel.*

Adventure Press Inc.
55 Jean-Talon Street West
Montreal, Quebec, Canada H2R 2W8
adventurepress.ca

Publisher: Marc G. Alain
Editorial Director: Marie-Eve Labelle
Author and illustrator: Alex A.
Page layout: Vicky Masse
Translator: Rhonda Mullins

Legal deposit – Bibliothèque et Archives nationales du Québec, 2016
Legal deposit – Library and Archives Canada, 2016

ISBN 978-1-77285-004-8 (PAPERBACK)

ISBN 978-1-77285-007-9 (PDF)
ISBN 978-1-77285-008-6 (EPUB)
ISBN 978-1-77285-009-3 (KINDLE)

We gratefully acknowledge the financial support of the Government of Canada through the Canada Book Fund (CBF) for our publishing activities.

Government of Quebec – Tax credit for book publishing and Business support program for books and specialized publishing – SODEC

Printed in China

TIME TRAVEL FRIDGE

WRITTEN AND ILLUSTRATED
BY ALEX A.

ADVENTURE PRESS

I'D LIKE TO DEDICATE THIS BOOK
TO MY DOG WHO FORCES ME
TO GO FOR WALKS AND TAKE A BREAK
WHEN I'M WORKING TOO HARD.

GOVERNMENT BUILDING, 12:13 PM.

ANALYZING FILE . . .
MISSION ACCOMPLISHED
FILE LOCATED. RETURN TO BASE.

IS ANYONE IN HERE?

OH WELL... THERE'S NO ONE HERE

CLAK

SNAP

ARE YOU SURE THERE WAS NO ONE?! MAYBE WE SHOULD TAKE ANOTHER LOOK.
NO. I CAN'T TAKE THE DISAPPOINTMENT, AGAIN...

ALEX A. PRESENTS

THE INTRUDER
IS IN THERE...
EXIT

GET HIM!
LOOK OUT, HE'S ARMED!!
SQUIRT
ARGH!!! HORRIBLY LUKEWARM!!!
BOING

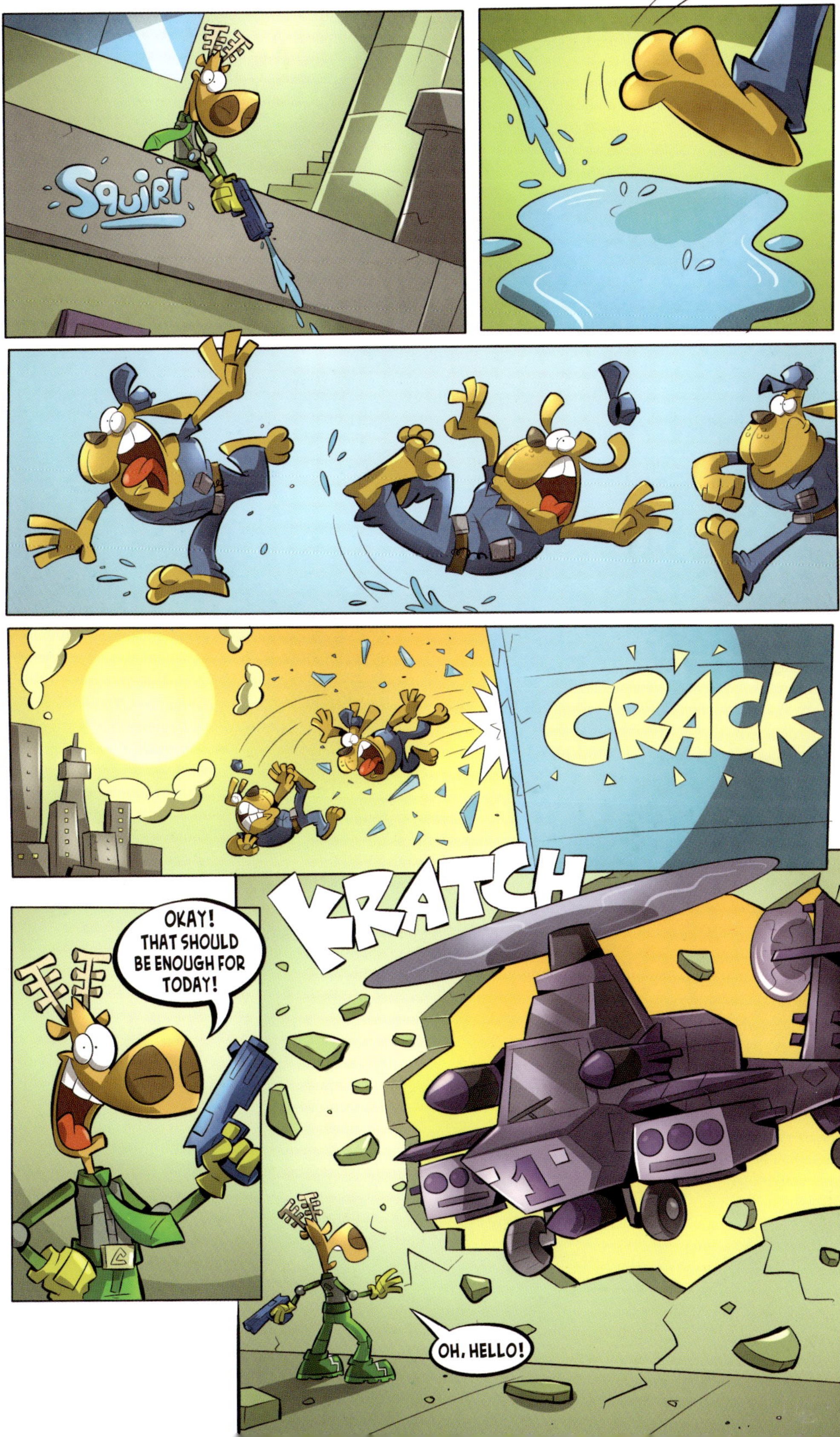

CRACK

KRATCH

OKAY! THAT SHOULD BE ENOUGH FOR TODAY!

OH, HELLO!

IN COOPERATION WITH ADVENTURE PRESS

!

HE'S GOING TO JUMP!
IS HE NUTS? DOESN'T HE KNOW ABOUT NEWTON'S LAW OF UNIVERSAL GRAVITATION?!?

VOLUME 5 OF THE ADVENTURES OF...

BOOM!

JON LE BON.

WHAT?!

JON LE BON!!!
AH! GOT iT. THANKS!

SUPER AGENT
JON LE BON!
5
TIME TRAVEL FRIDGE

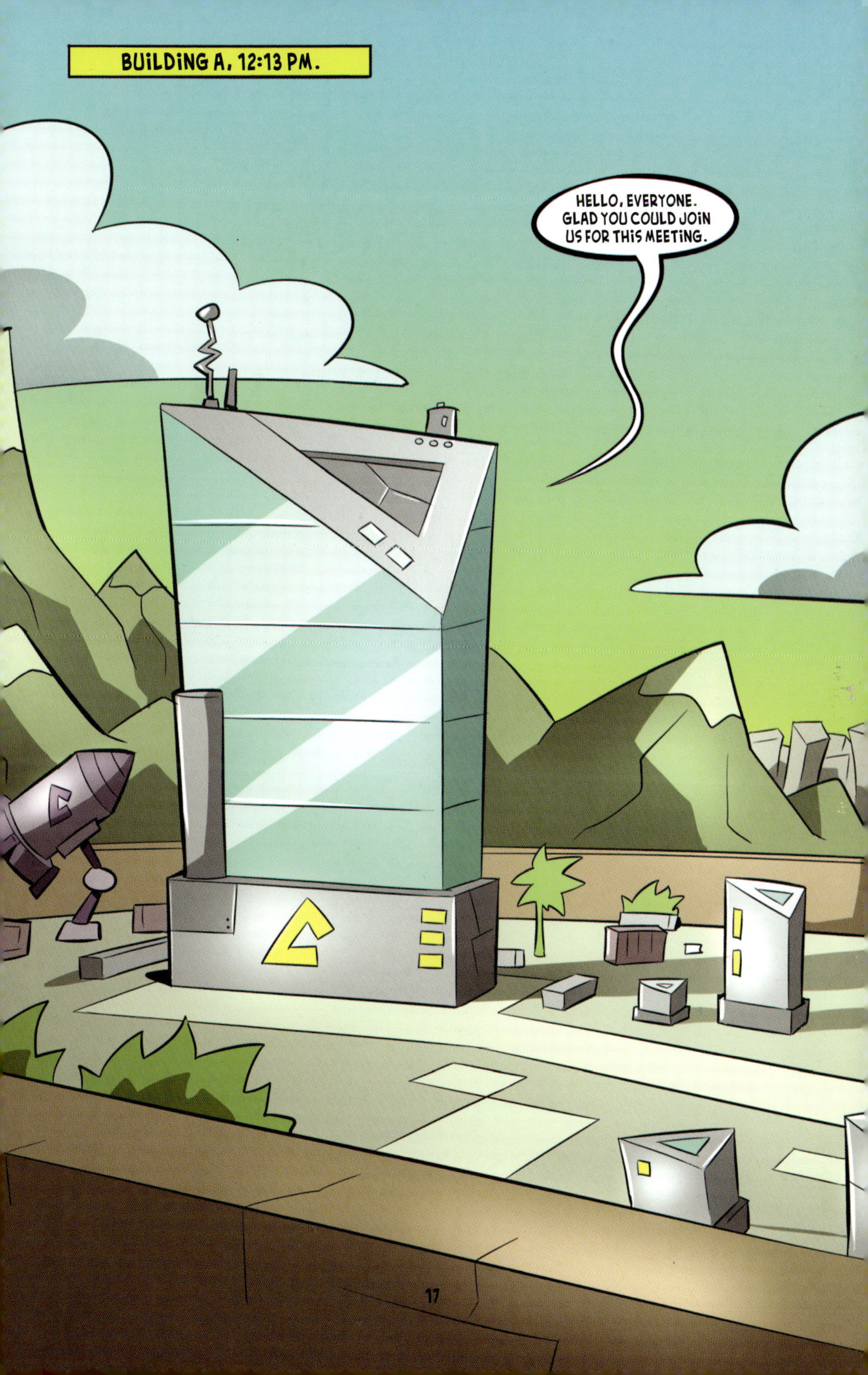

BUILDING A, 12:13 PM.

SO, WHAT'S THE WORLD SITUATION THIS WEEK?
NOTHING TO REPORT IN K SECTOR, AS ALWAYS.
F SECTOR TOO. IT'S AS DULL AS IT SEEMS.
WE HAD TO REPEL AN ATTACK OF WHAT WAS LEFT OF WHITEWASH'S MONSTERS. THE SITUATION IS NOW UNDER CONTROL.
AND WHAT ABOUT YOU, MARTHA? DID YOU FIND ANY TRACE OF CASSANDRA?
STILL NOTHING. WE'RE ABOUT TO CALL OFF THE SEARCH.
BUT WE DID MANAGE TO CAPTURE HER SON AND HER HENCHMAN.

WE'LL BE STARTING THEIR REHABILITATION SOON.
SPEAKING OF WHICH, HOW IS WORK GOING ON THE INTRANEURONAL 3000?
WE SHOULD COMPLETE THE PROGRAMMING IN A MONTH.

HOSTILIA, THE DANGEROUS SCIENTIST, IS THE ONLY ONE STILL ON THE RUN.
IT'S IMPORTANT THAT WE FIND HER. HER ARMY OF BLOODTHIRSTY BANANAS COULD BECOME A PROBLEM IF SHE KEEPS GROWING.

VERY GOOD. I'M GOING TO SIGN OFF. I HAVE A LOT OF WORK TO DO.
OH, BEFORE YOU DO, MA'AM, IS THERE ANY WORD ABOUT...

BIG BEAVER?

NOW CUT THAT OUT!
BIG BEAVER IS DEAD FOR HEAVEN'S SAKE! ANYONE COULD HAVE BUILT THAT ROBOT THEY BROUGHT BACK FROM THE REDLANDS.
OF COURSE. THESE DAYS IT'S EASY TO BUILD A PERFECT ROBOT.

... NO, WE STILL HAVEN'T FOUND ANYTHING. BUT IF HE'S THE ONE WHO SENT THAT ROBOT, IT'S CLEARLY TO CAUSE PANIC IN THE AGENCY.
LET'S NOT GIVE IN TO IT. LET'S KEEP OUR HEADS.

TZ
TZZZZ
BUILDING A, OVER AND OUT.

JUMP, FILIPO!
HOW CAN I WASTE THREE HOURS OF MY LIFE TRYING TO JUMP ON A PLATFORM?!

BILLY! I TOLD YOU TO FINISH INSPECTING THE COMPUTER NETWORK!
IT'S DONE, MA'AM. NO TRACE OF NETWORK INTRUSION SINCE THE ATTACK BY HENRY'S BRAIN. THE SYSTEM IS AS CLEAN AS IT APPEARS.
I CHECKED IT THREE TIMES.

THANK YOU. WHAT LEVEL ARE YOU AT?
12. I CAN'T GET TO THE OTHER SIDE OF THE FLAG.
USE THE DINOSAUR AND GO UNDER IT.

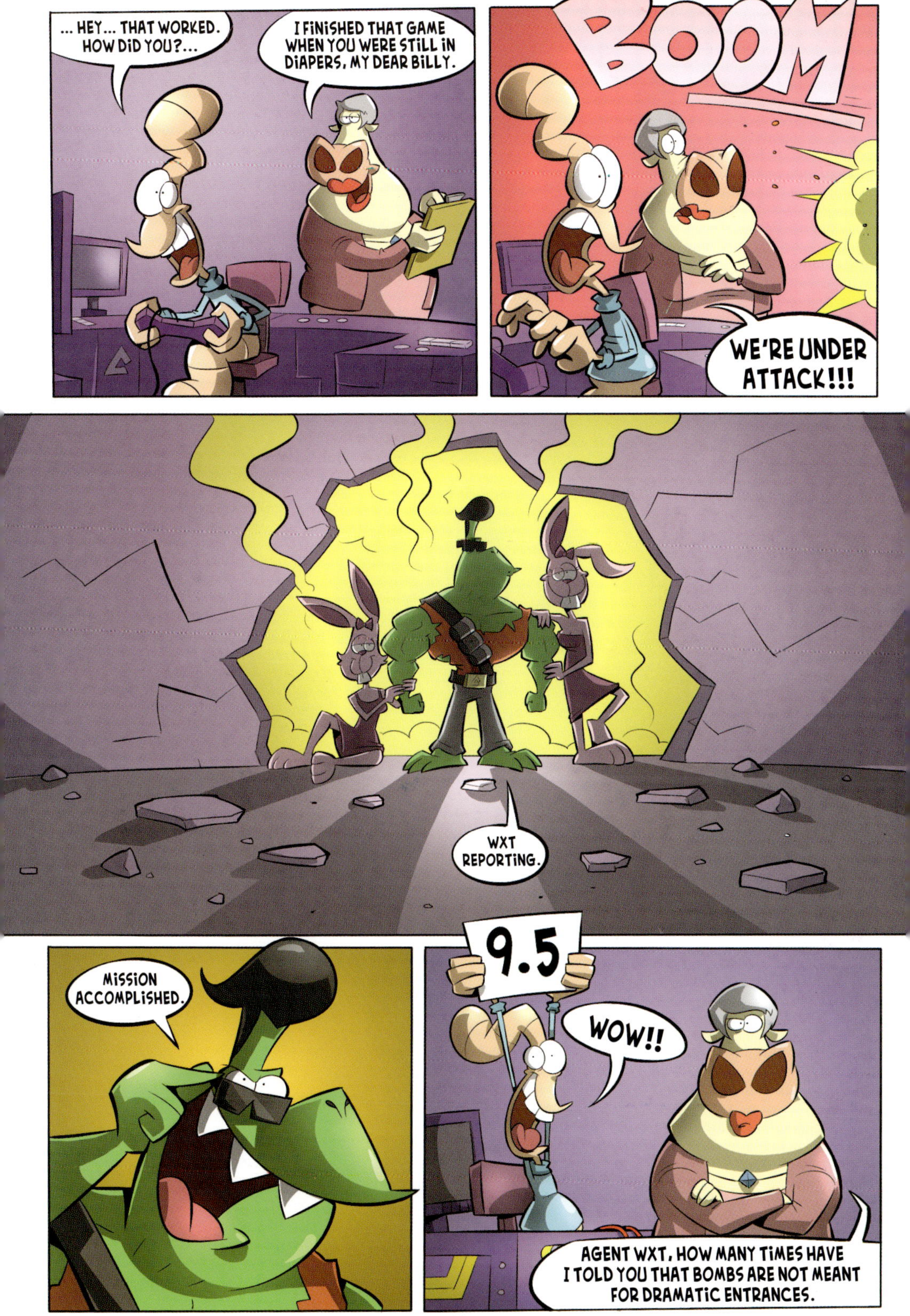

WXT REPORTING.

MISSION ACCOMPLISHED.

9.5

WOW!!

AGENT WXT, HOW MANY TIMES HAVE I TOLD YOU THAT BOMBS ARE NOT MEANT FOR DRAMATIC ENTRANCES.

HEY! THE REASON I'M TOP DOG HERE ISN'T JUST BECAUSE OF MY SUCCESSFUL MISSIONS, IT'S FOR MY ENTRANCES TOO, ISN'T IT?
WE'RE UNDER ATTACK AGAIN!!!
CRACK

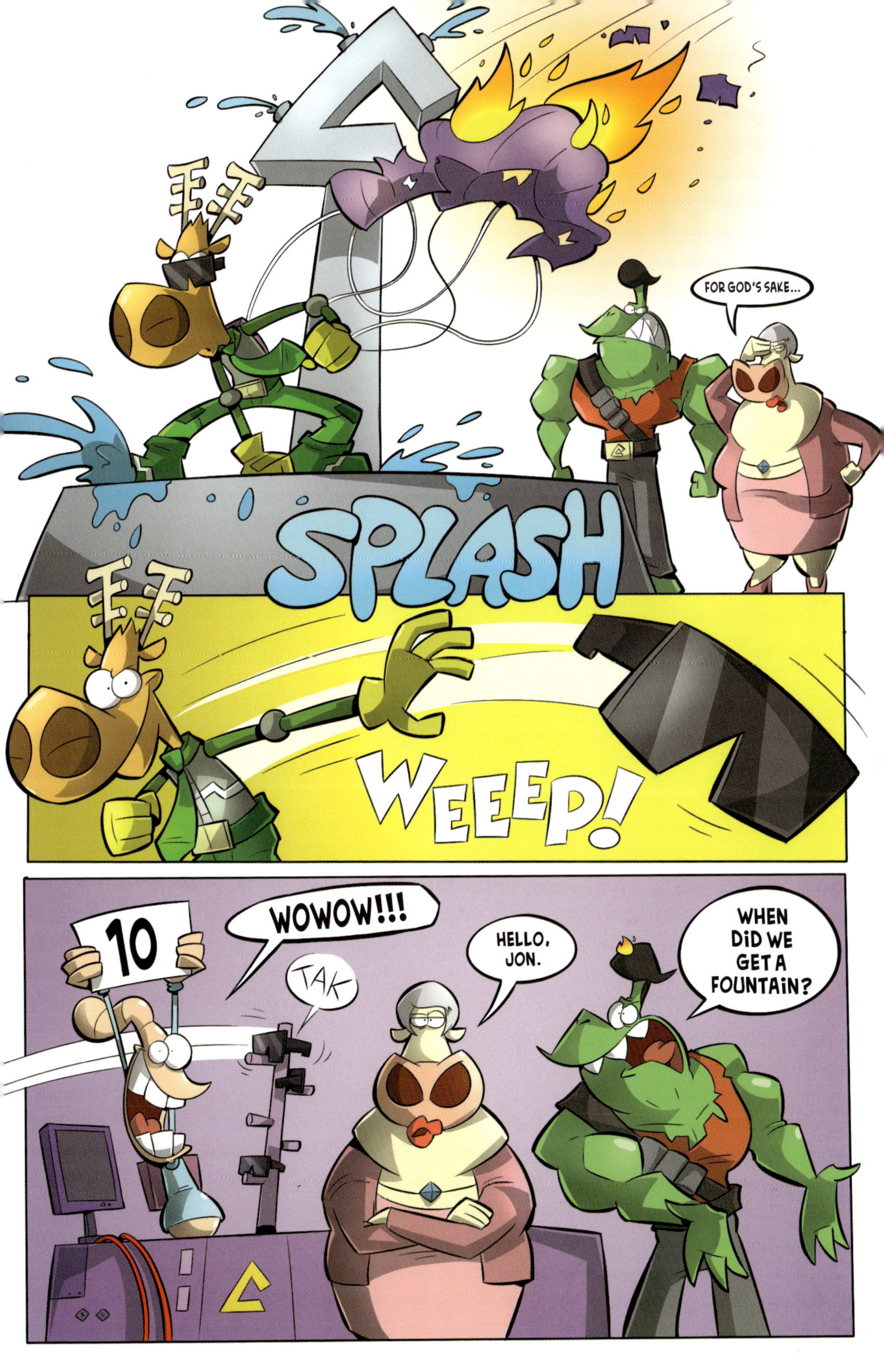

FOR GOD'S SAKE...

SPLASH

WEEEP!

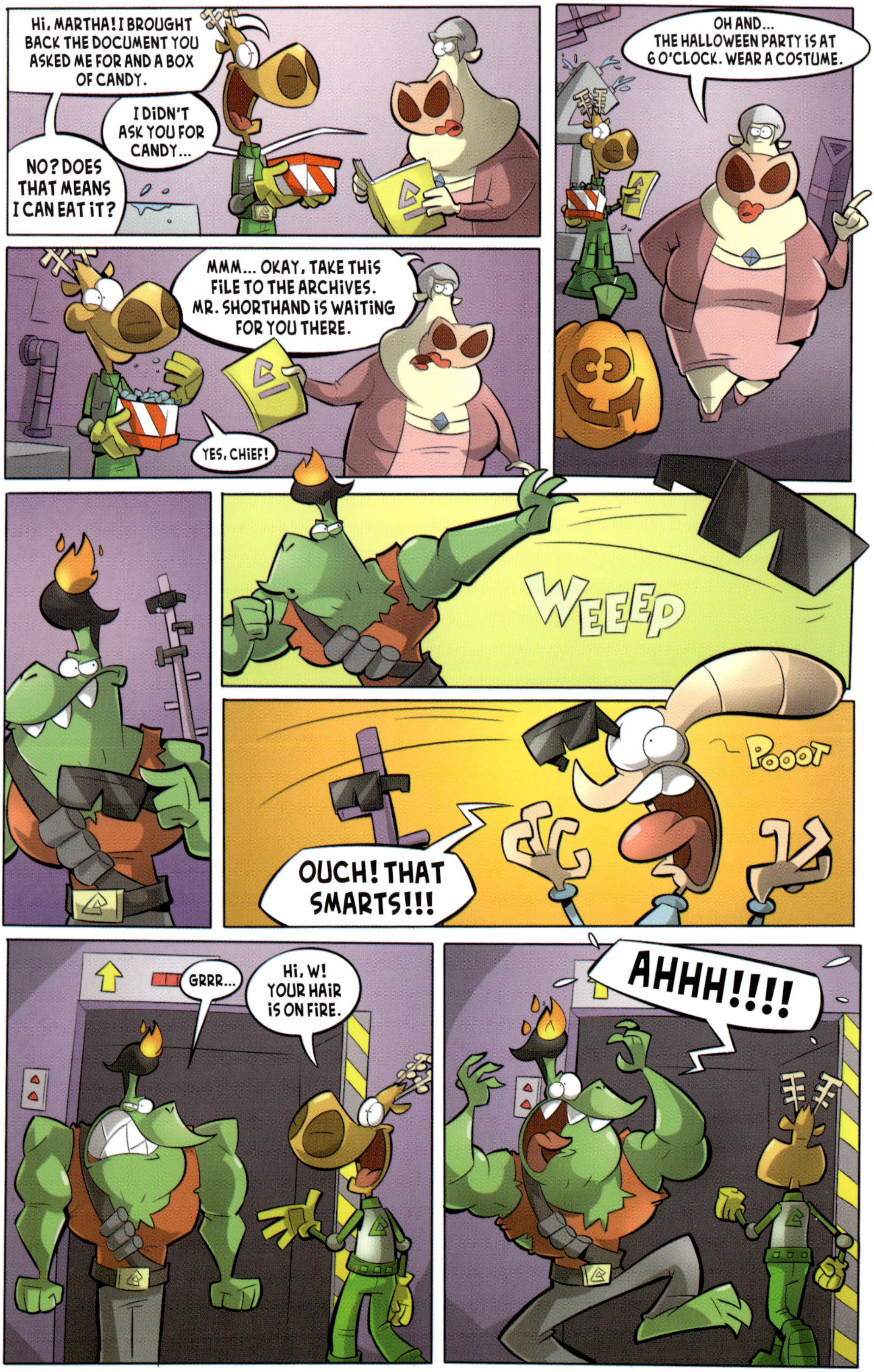

HI, MARTHA! I BROUGHT BACK THE DOCUMENT YOU ASKED ME FOR AND A BOX OF CANDY.

I DIDN'T ASK YOU FOR CANDY...

NO? DOES THAT MEANS I CAN EAT IT?

OH AND... THE HALLOWEEN PARTY IS AT 6 O'CLOCK. WEAR A COSTUME.

MMM... OKAY, TAKE THIS FILE TO THE ARCHIVES. MR. SHORTHAND IS WAITING FOR YOU THERE.

YES, CHIEF!

WEEEP

POOOT

OUCH! THAT SMARTS!!!

ARCHIVES.
I FOUND IT! FILE NUMBER 8642-A!
THANKS, THEODORE. ONLY 40,000 MORE TO GO.
THAT EARTHQUAKE REALLY DID SOME DAMAGE.
OH, NOT TO WORRY. IT'LL JUST TAKE PATIENCE.
SAY, YOU GET BY PRETTY WELL WITHOUT HANDS. WAS IT HARD HAVING TO GIVE UP BEING AN AGENT?
YES, PRETTY HARD. BUT I LIKE MY NEW JOB, AND WE KNEW THE RISKS WHEN WE SIGNED ON.
AND WERE YOU REALLY STUCK UNDER A PILE OF RUBBLE FOR 20 YEARS?
YEP!...
BUT AT LEAST I CAN STILL SCRATCH MY BUM.
TWINNN
AH! MY FILES!!

WE'VE TOLD YOU TO BE CAREFUL, HENRY. NEED I REMIND YOU THAT IT'S YOUR FAULT ONE OF OUR SECRET FILES GOT OUT OF THE BUILDING?

BUT I HAVE TO CONTINUE MY RESEARCH ON MICRO BLACK HOLES.

THANKS.
I'M THIS CLOSE TO BEING ABLE TO MANIPULATE DARK ENERGY TOO!
YA, YA... BUT IF YOU COULD WAIT UNTIL I'VE FINISHED RECLASSIFYING MY FILES, I WOULD APPRECIATE IT.
HEEEE!!!
WHAT NOW?!
NO! NO! ARGH! COULD YOU HAVE YOUR NERVOUS BREAKDOWN OVER THERE? PLEASE?
PAP
LET'S GET OUT OF HERE! HE'S COMING BACK!
HUH?

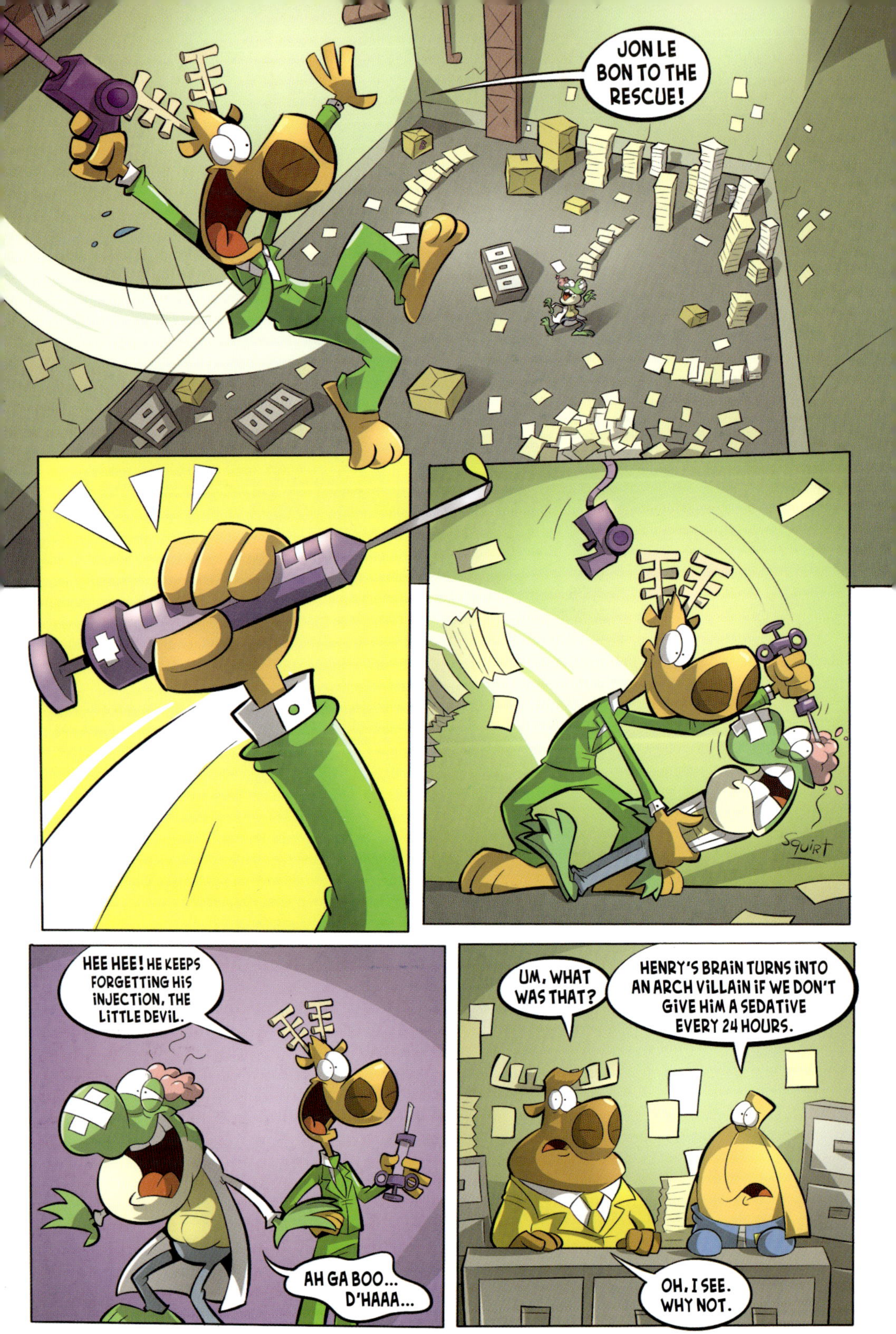

JON LE BON TO THE RESCUE!

SQUIRT

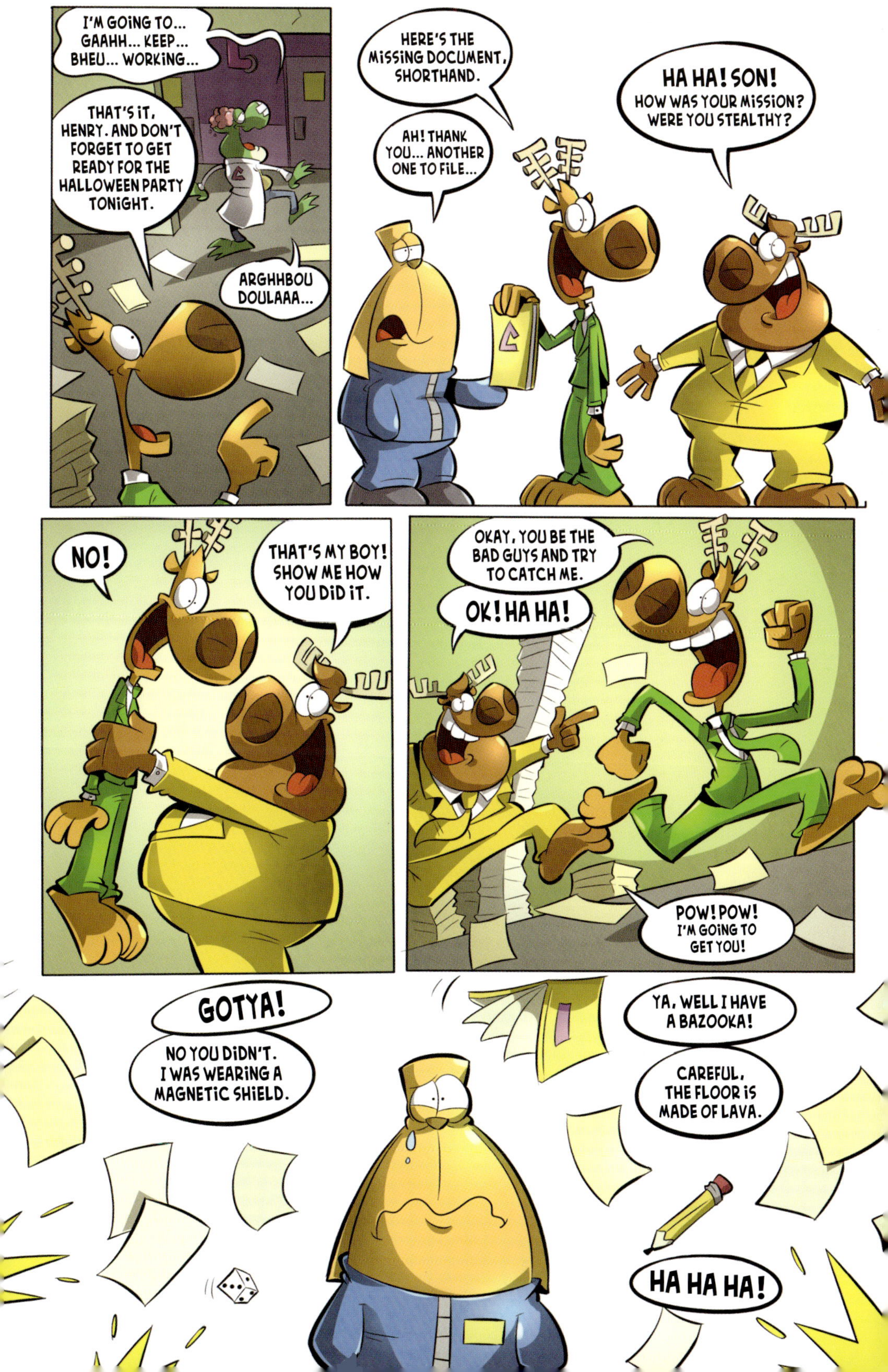

I'M GOING TO... GAAHH... KEEP... BHEU... WORKING...
THAT'S IT, HENRY. AND DON'T FORGET TO GET READY FOR THE HALLOWEEN PARTY TONIGHT.
ARGHHBOU DOULAAA...

HERE'S THE MISSING DOCUMENT, SHORTHAND.
AH! THANK YOU... ANOTHER ONE TO FILE...
HA HA! SON! HOW WAS YOUR MISSION? WERE YOU STEALTHY?

YA, WELL I HAVE A BAZOOKA!
CAREFUL, THE FLOOR IS MADE OF LAVA.

OH! I JUST REMEMBERED IT'S TIME FOR ME TO WORK OUT WITH WXT. SEE YOU TONIGHT!
BYE, BYE!

DO YOU WANT ME TO HELP YOU FINISH??
BOO HOO HOO HOO!!!

AND... THREE... COME ON, PUT YOUR BACK INTO IT!

WOOF! I'M A LITTLE OUT OF SHAPE.
COME ON, I THINK YOU'RE STILL IN GREAT SHAPE.

YA, BUT I DON'T HAVE YOUR ABS. IS IT TRUE THAT YOU CAN GRATE CHEESE ON THEM?
JUST MOZZARELLA.
THAT'S HANDY.

IS IT ME OR DO YOU SEEM A BIT BASHFUL WITH ME?

HMM. SORRY, IT'S JUST THAT... WELL, I DIDN'T HAVE THE NERVE TO TELL YOU BUT... YOU'RE MY IDOL...
SERIOUSLY? BUT YOU WERE ONLY TEN YEARS OLD WHEN I WENT MISSING!
YES, BUT MARTHA HAD ME READ LOTS OF STUFF ABOUT YOU, ABOUT EVERYTHING YOU ACCOMPLISHED, AND...
IT INSPIRED ME. EVER SINCE, I'VE BEEN DOING EVERYTHING I CAN TO BECOME LIKE YOU.
TO BECOME THE BEST.
HA HA! THAT'S WONDERFUL! AND BASED ON WHAT I'VE HEARD ABOUT YOU, YOU'RE DOING PRETTY WELL.
YA, BUT... NOT AS WELL AS YOUR SON.
I TOLD YOU I COULD GET MY FOREARMS UP MY NOSE!!!
UM, I NEVER SAID YOU COULDN'T.
SO? THE JOB ISN'T A COMPETITION, YOU KNOW. YOU LOVE WHAT YOU DO, DON'T YOU?
YA... BUT...
BEING THE BEST ISN'T WHAT'S IMPORTANT.
THAT'S EASY ENOUGH TO SAY WHEN YOU'RE A LIVING LEGEND.
MMM, TRUE, TRUE.

BUT... I DON'T KNOW...
I GET THE FEELING THAT I'LL NEVER ACHIEVE MY GOALS EVEN THOUGH I'M DOING EVERYTHING I CAN.
DO YOU HAVE ANY ADVICE FOR ME?

DO YOUR JOB FOR THE RIGHT REASONS... AND YOU'LL BE THE BEST.

AND NEVER FREEZE MEAT THAT'S ALREADY BEEN FROZEN. IT FORMS BACTERIA.
HUH?

THEY'RE IN THE BUILDING, SIR.
PERFECT. READY THE TANKS.

IT'S TIME FOR A LITTLE CHAT.

HAPPY HALLOWEEN
UM, AS COSTUMES GO, IT'S HARDLY A STRETCH.
WHAT ARE YOU TALKING ABOUT? I HAD TO WORK OUT FOR THREE MONTHS!
ARRGHHHH!
HULK, NOT HAPPY!
CRACK
MMM... THAT WOULD NEVER HAVE HAPPENED TO THE REAL HULK!

I DON'T UNDERSTAND YOUR COSTUME...
IT'S OBVIOUS, ISN'T IT? I'VE SIMULATED AN UNSTABLE STRUCTURE OF MY BODY'S ATOMS TO PRETEND THAT PART OF ME HAS DISAPPEARED INTO ANOTHER DIMENSION!
PRETTY COOL, EH!?
YA, IT'S OKAY... I'M A JAR OF JAM.

CAN I HAVE YOUR ATTENTION, EVERYONE? IT'S TIME TO ANNOUNCE THE WINNER OF THIS YEAR'S COSTUME CONTEST.

WHAT DO WE WIN?
NOT DINNER WITH BILLY AGAIN?
YOU DIDN'T LIKE THAT?

NO, A NEXT-GENERATION VIDEO GAME CONSOLE!
HD, WI-FI, WITH A TOUCH-SCREEN JOYSTICK AND THE NEW TURBO FILIPO! A LITTLE SOMETHING TO HELP YOU WHILE AWAY THE TIME AT WORK.
OOO!

AND THE WINNER IS...
BILLY!

WHAT?!
I SPENT THREE YEARS WORKING ON MY COSTUME!!!
FANTASTIC! JON, HOW ABOUT A GAME OF TURBO FILIPO AFTER THE PARTY?
YOU BET!
CONGRATULATIONS, BILLY. THE JURY ENJOYED THE IRONY BEHIND YOUR COSTUME.
BOOO!
BEEP BEEP BEEP BEEP
MULTIPLE INTRUSIONS ON OUR TERRITORY, MA'AM.
IT LOOKS LIKE... TANKS!
I'LL HANDLE THIS.

WHO ARE YOU AND WHAT DO YOU WANT?!
... I ASKED YOU A QUESTiON.

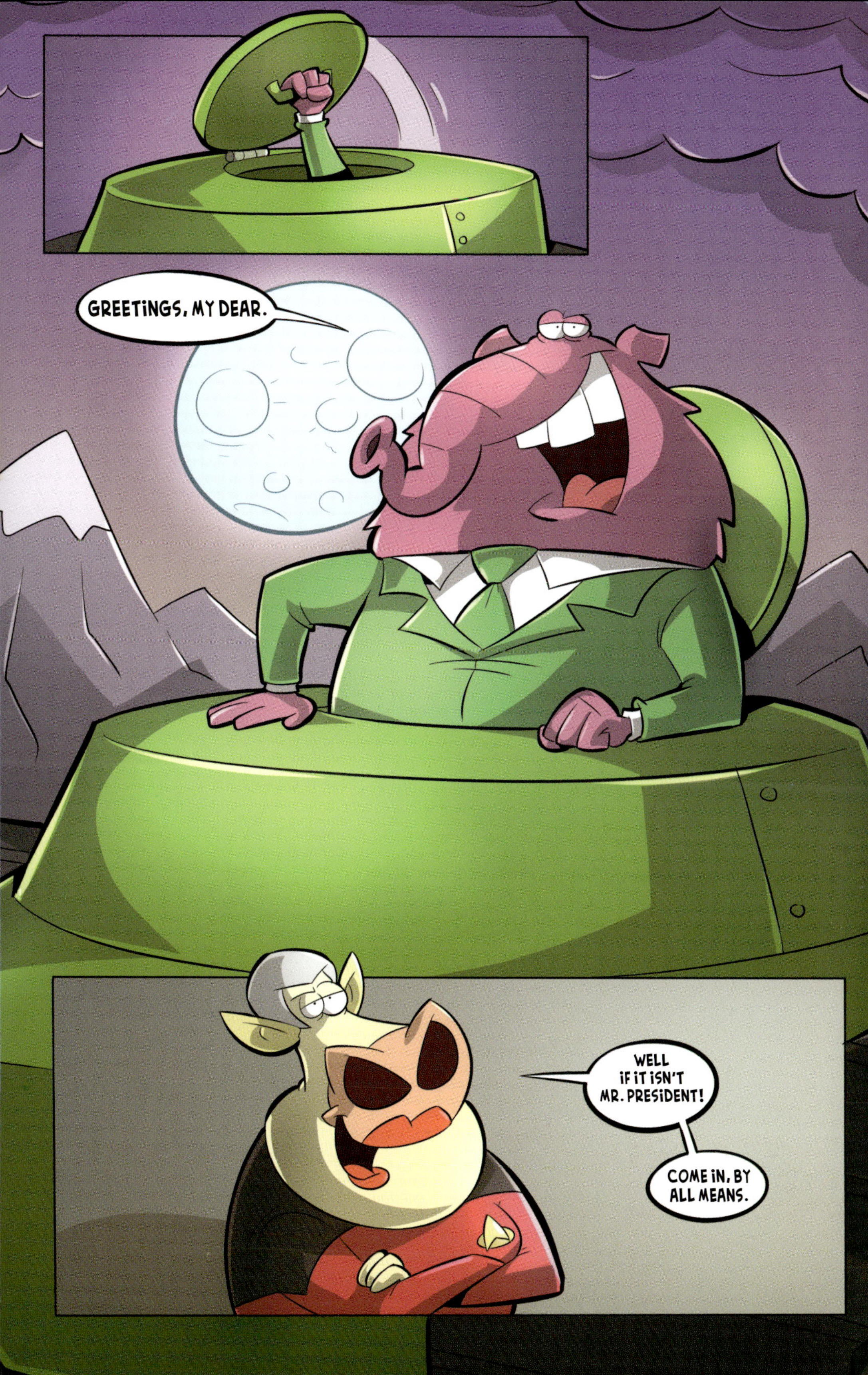
GREETINGS, MY DEAR.
WELL IF IT ISN'T MR. PRESIDENT!
COME IN, BY ALL MEANS.

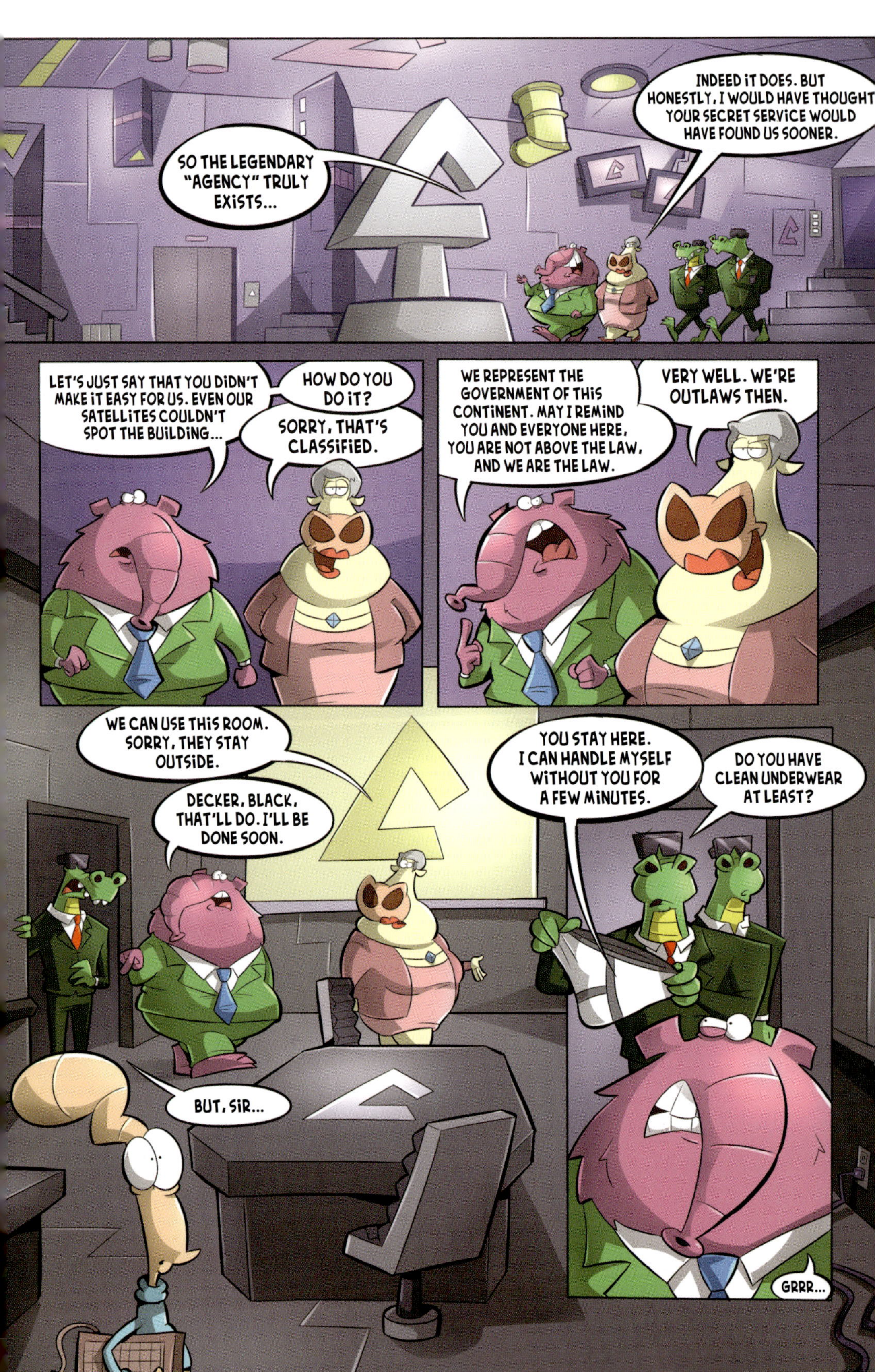
SO THE LEGENDARY "AGENCY" TRULY EXISTS...
INDEED iT DOES. BUT HONESTLY, I WOULD HAVE THOUGHT YOUR SECRET SERViCE WOULD HAVE FOUND US SOONER.
LET'S JUST SAY THAT YOU DiDN'T MAKE iT EASY FOR US. EVEN OUR SATELLiTES COULDN'T SPOT THE BUiLDiNG...
HOW DO YOU DO iT?
SORRY, THAT'S CLASSiFiED.
WE REPRESENT THE GOVERNMENT OF THiS CONTiNENT. MAY I REMiND YOU AND EVERYONE HERE, YOU ARE NOT ABOVE THE LAW, AND WE ARE THE LAW.
VERY WELL. WE'RE OUTLAWS THEN.
WE CAN USE THiS ROOM. SORRY, THEY STAY OUTSiDE.
DECKER, BLACK, THAT'LL DO. I'LL BE DONE SOON.
BUT, SiR...
YOU STAY HERE. I CAN HANDLE MYSELF WiTHOUT YOU FOR A FEW MiNUTES.
DO YOU HAVE CLEAN UNDERWEAR AT LEAST?
GRRR...

SO, WHAT BRINGS YOU?
I HAVE DOCUMENTS ON THIS KEY THAT EXPLAIN THE SITUATION. WHERE CAN I PLUG IT IN?
BILLY, WOULD YOU PLEASE?
YES, MA'AM!

TIDOOM

UM, THIS COMPUTER IS AT LEAST TEN YEARS OLD... THIS WILL TAKE A FEW MINUTES.

OKAY, LET'S CHAT A LITTLE. WHAT EXACTLY DO YOU DO IN THIS BUILDING?
ASSUMING THIS IS THE ONLY ONE YOU HAVE...

WITH THE NUMBER OF BUILDINGS WE HAVE, I'M SURPRISED YOU FOUND ONLY THIS ONE.

DON'T WORRY, MR. PRESIDENT. OUR INTENTIONS ARE PEACEFUL.
LIKE WHEN WE DECIDED TO DISARM YOUR NUCLEAR WEAPONS.

THAT WAS YOU? I THOUGHT IT WAS ALIENS.

YOU AND I BOTH KNOW THAT ALIENS MIND THEIR OWN BUSINESS.

AND WHAT GIVES YOU THE RIGHT TO MESS AROUND IN THE BUSINESS OF OTHERS?
DO YOU THINK YOU OWN THIS PLANET?

WE'RE JUST HERE TO PREVENT ITS SELF-DESTRUCTION. IF YOU ONLY KNEW THE NUMBER OF TIMES WE PREVENTED THE END OF THE WORLD.

SO YOU THINK THAT WITHOUT YOU, EARTHLINGS WOULD HAVE BEEN WIPED OUT?

I DON'T THINK IT.
I KNOW IT.

AND HOW DO YOU FINANCE ALL THIS? WHERE DO YOU GET THE MONEY? YOU STEAL IT FROM US, IS THAT IT?
YOU THINK YOU'RE ALL ROBIN HOODS?

HA HA!
WE ARE COMPLETELY SELF-SUFFICIENT, I CAN ASSURE YOU. MONEY DOESN'T HAVE MUCH VALUE HERE.

AND WHAT ABOUT ENERGY? IT'S NOT AS THOUGH A BUILDING LIKE THIS RUNS ON BATTERIES.

THAT'S ALSO CONFIDENTIAL. BUT, EVEN IF I EXPLAINED IT, I DON'T THINK YOU WOULD UNDERSTAND.

SO YOU'RE HIDING ADVANCED TECHNOLOGY FROM THE WORLD. THIS JUST KEEPS GETTING BETTER.

PEOPLE AREN'T READY FOR CERTAIN TECHNOLOGY.

HA HA! WHAT ARE YOU SAYING? EARTHLINGS AREN'T EVOLVED ENOUGH TO PLAY WITH YOUR TOYS? THEY'RE STILL CHILDREN, IS THAT IT?

YES, THAT'S WHAT I THINK.

... AND HOW ARE YOU ANY BETTER?

WE'VE BEEN HERE LONGER.

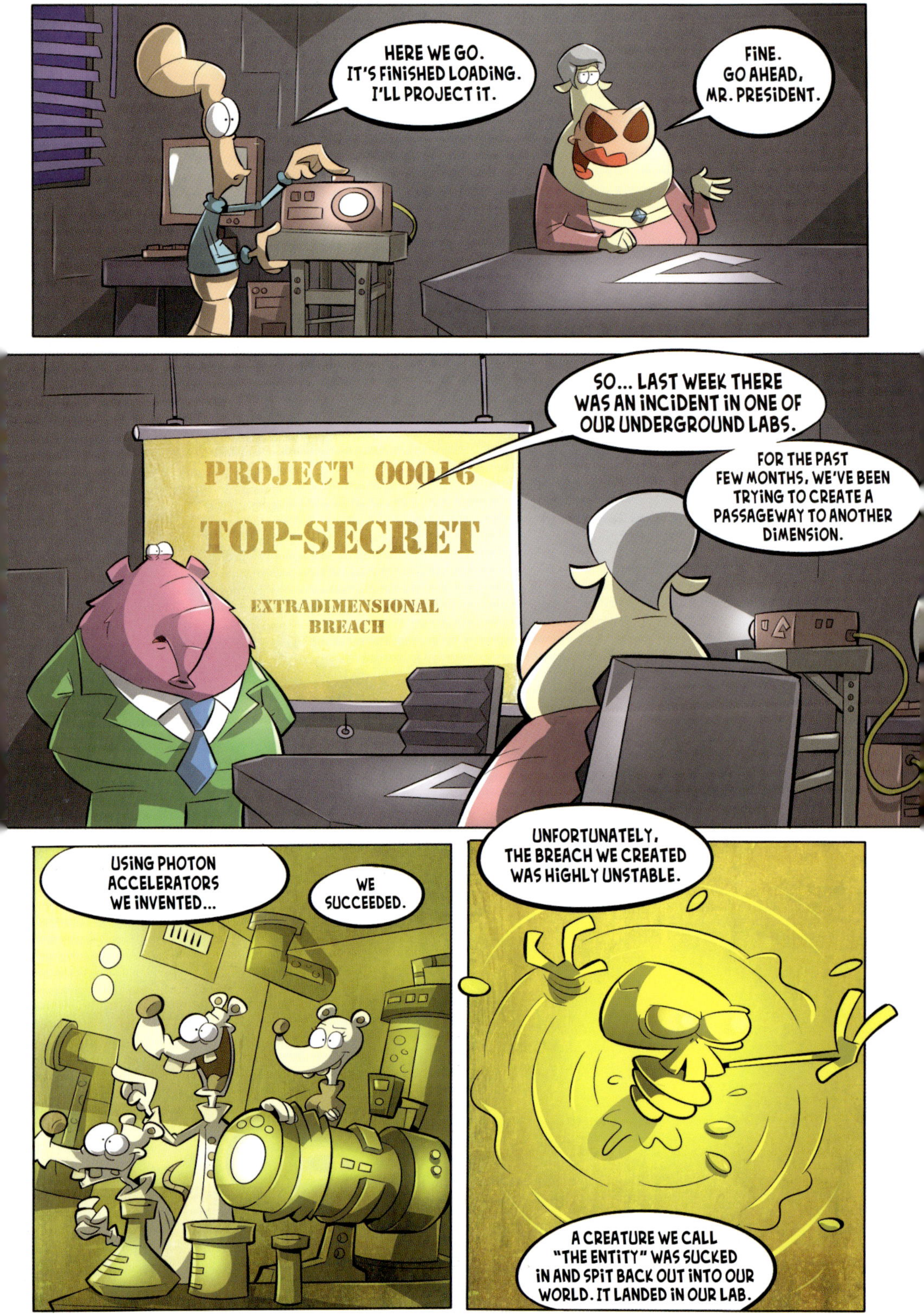

PROJECT 00016
TOP-SECRET
EXTRADIMENSIONAL BREACH
SO... LAST WEEK THERE WAS AN INCIDENT IN ONE OF OUR UNDERGROUND LABS.
FOR THE PAST FEW MONTHS, WE'VE BEEN TRYING TO CREATE A PASSAGEWAY TO ANOTHER DIMENSION.

VISIBLY HOSTILE, THIS... MONSTER DESTROYED EVERYTHING AND ESCAPED ON A RAY OF LIGHT, TAKING WITH HIM...

MY DAUGHTER MAPLE...
WHO WAS NEARBY AT THE TIME.

OH, THAT'S NOT COOL.
ACCORDING TO OUR SCIENTIFIC DATA, WHICH FOLLOWED THE CREATURE'S ENERGY TRAIL, IT TELETRANSPORTED SOMEWHERE ON EARTH...

200,000
YEARS AGO.

A CREATURE THAT CAN TIME TRAVEL? INTERESTING. AND... WHAT EXACTLY DO YOU WANT FROM US?

WELL I KNOW YOU DEVELOP SECRET TECHNOLOGY TOO, AND THAT YOU MAY EVEN BE MORE ADVANCED THAN US. SO MY QUESTION IS... CAN YOU HELP US TRAVEL BACK IN TIME?
IT'S POSSIBLE, BUT WHY WOULD WE DO THAT FOR YOU?

UM, DON'T YOU WANT TO HELP A POOR GRIEVING FATHER?

I TOLD YOU, WE DON'T INTERFERE IN PEOPLE'S LIVES UNLESS THE FATE OF THE WORLD IS AT STAKE.
MA'AM, THE TIME LINE COULD BE PROFOUNDLY AFFECTED BY THIS, COULDN'T IT?

HE'S RIGHT. SOME OF MY SCIENTISTS HAVE ADVANCED THE THEORY THAT THE MERE PRESENCE OF THIS CREATURE IN OUR REALITY WOULD CAUSE MAJOR DISRUPTIONS IN THE FABRIC OF TIME.
I DON'T SEE ANY EVIDENCE OF THAT RIGHT NOW.

BUT LOOK, HE HAS AN ARM COMING OUT OF HIS HEAD!
HE'S ALWAYS HAD THAT ARM.
HE HAS A POINT.

AND LOOK OUTSIDE!

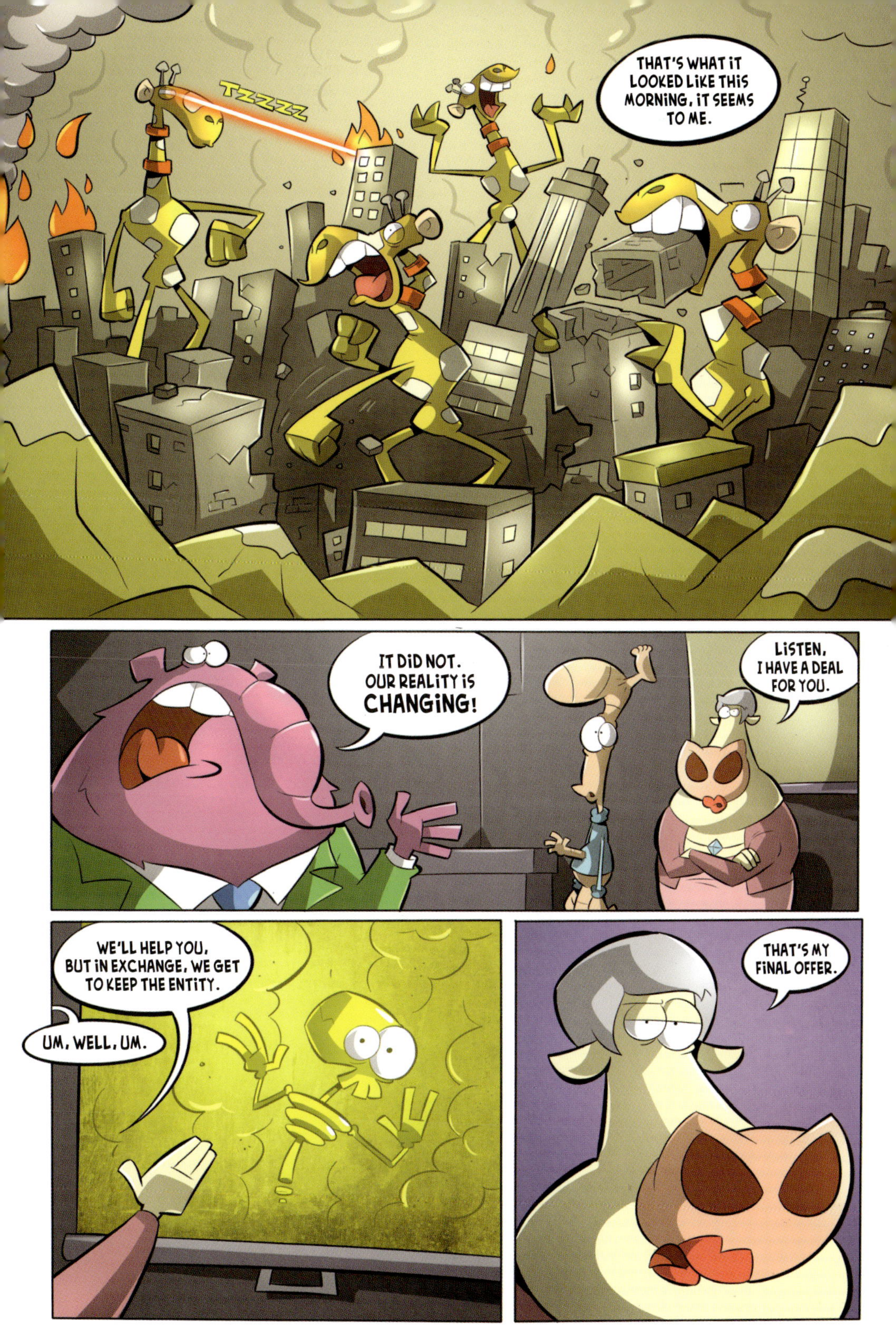

TZZZZZ

THAT'S WHAT IT LOOKED LIKE THIS MORNING, IT SEEMS TO ME.

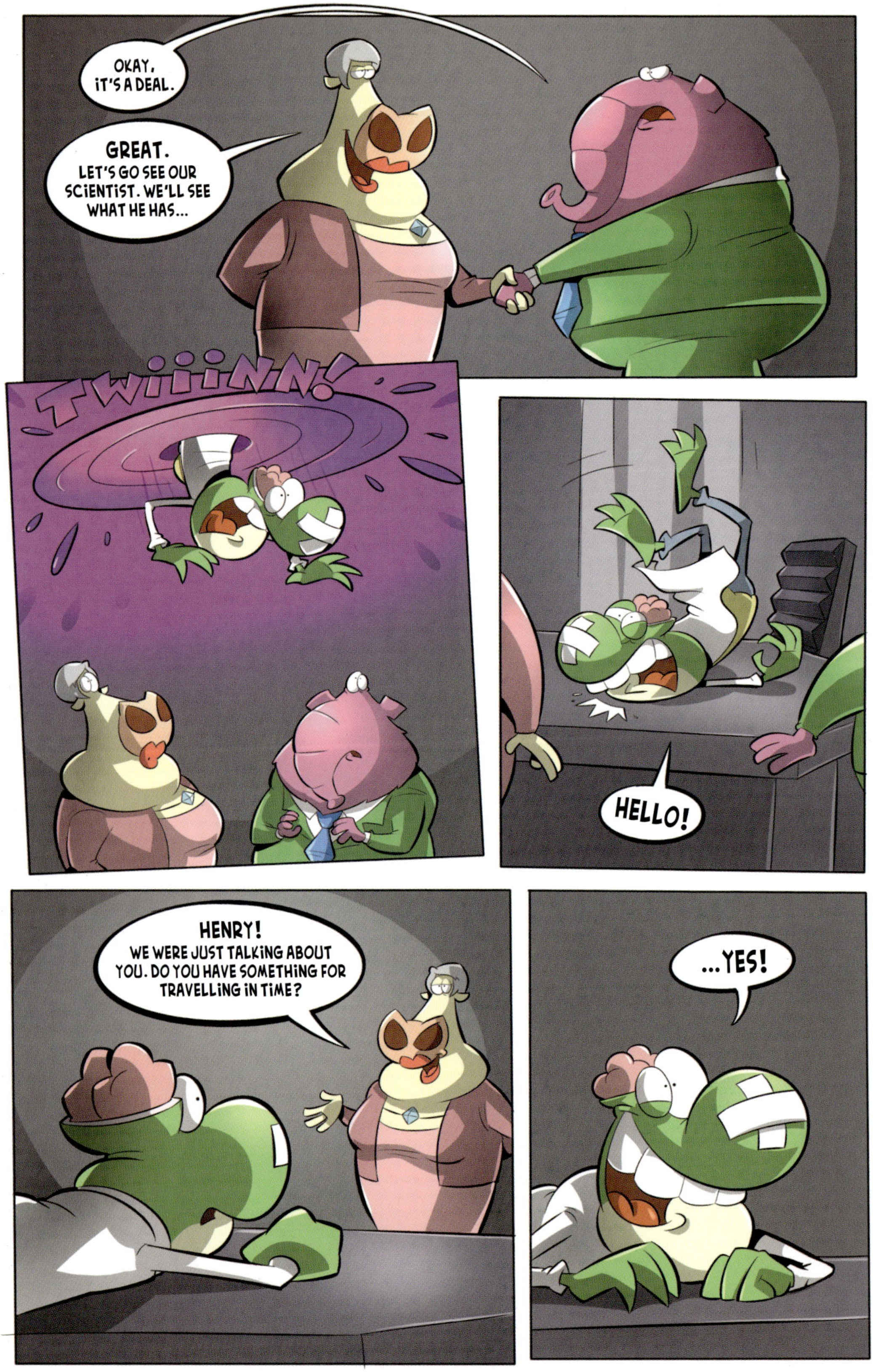

OKAY, IT'S A DEAL.
GREAT. LET'S GO SEE OUR SCIENTIST. WE'LL SEE WHAT HE HAS...
TWIIINNN!
HELLO!

PRESENTING...
THE TIME TRAVEL FRIDGE!
I BEG YOUR PARDON?
CAN YOU EXPLAIN HOW IT WORKS?
OF COURSE, YOU SEE...
HEY MARTHA! WHAT'S WITH ALL THE TANKS IN FRONT...?
YOU!
YOU?!
ARGH!

YOU PUT ME AND MY FRIENDS iN PRiSON!
QAF
KRAK
FLOOSH
KiF
YOU BETRAYED THE ARMY OF THE FiRST CONTiNENT!
HEY! I WANT iN ON THiS!

YiPPEE!
POOF

THAT'S ENOUGH!

HEE HEE! LET'S DO iT AGAiN!
SO THIS IS WHERE YOU'VE BEEN HiDiNG ALL THESE YEARS, WITH THESE ANARCHiSTS! YOU KNOW, MA'AM, THiS MAN BETRAYED HiS HOMELAND, ESCAPED FROM PRiSON AND HAS BEEN WANTED FOR MORE THAN 30 YEARS.
MMMM, SORT OF LiKE EVERYONE HERE, YES!

GRRR...

HELLO! I'M JON!
AND HE'S REPRODUCING TOO...
OKAY, OKAY, CAN WE GET BACK TO HENRY, PLEASE? HE WAS GOING TO EXPLAIN HOW HIS TIME TRAVEL MACHINE WORKS.
HA! YOU INVENTED A TIME TRAVEL MACHINE?! CAN I TRY???
I WANT TO GO BACK 10 YEARS IN THE PAST TO SEE WHETHER IT'S TRUE THAT MY NOSTRILS HAVE GROWN TO RIDICULOUS PROPORTIONS.
I CAN ASSURE YOU THEY HAVE.
SO... IT ALL STARTED WHEN JON BROUGHT THIS BACK FROM A MISSION.
IT'S THE TOASTER OF THE GODS!
PRECISELY. THIS MACHINE IS USED MAINLY TO TRAVEL TO THE PAST, BUT IT ONLY LETS YOU GO BACK FIVE MINUTES. SO I TOOK IT APART TO TRY TO UNDERSTAND HOW IT WORKS.
AND THAT'S WHEN I FOUND...

THIS.
IT'S BASICALLY ITS FUEL. IT'S SUCH DENSELY CONCENTRATED PHOTONS THAT YOU MIGHT CALL IT...
... LIQUID LIGHT.
WOWWWW...
HOW MUCH ENERGY IS IN THERE?
AROUND SIX TIMES THE ENERGY OF OUR SUN.
OKAY, SO I GUESS IT WOULD BE A GOOD IDEA TO KEEP THIS A SECRET.
ONCE I DISCOVERED THIS VIRTUALLY UNLIMITED FORM OF ENERGY, I WANTED TO BUILD A BIGGER MACHINE THAT COULD HANDLE A LONG TRIP, AND THAT'S WHEN I THOUGHT OF A FRIDGE.
IT ALLOWS YOU TO TRAVEL OVER 600,000 YEARS INTO THE PAST OR THE FUTURE!
SO THAT'S PERFECT THEN!
B+

WHY A FRIDGE?
OH, I SAW A MOVIE THAT SAID IT COULD WITHSTAND A NUCLEAR BLAST, SO...
B+

AND IT WORKS?
IN THEORY, YES, BUT I HAVEN'T TESTED IT ON PEOPLE...
WHO WANTS TO TRY?

STAND BACK. WHETHER IT MEANS TRAVELLING TO THE PAST OR THE FUTURE, INTO SPACE OR TO THE OCEAN FLOOR, OR EVEN TO THE OUTER LIMITS OF THE UNIVERSE, WXT IS HERE.
AND MY HAIR WILL STAY IN PLACE.
OOO! OOO!
VERY WELL, LET'S PROCEED!

FIFTEEN MINUTES LATER.
COULDN'T YOU HAVE MADE YOUR TIME MACHINE A LITTLE BIGGER?!
...WE INTELLECTUALS RARELY FACTOR IN MUSCLES.
SORRY, AGENT WXT, YOU CAN'T COMPLETE THIS MISSION. JON WILL DO IT INSTEAD.

HA HA! YOU'RE FAT!
GRRR...
NOT TRUE, YOU'RE VERY HANDSOME.

YOU HAVE FIVE MINUTES TO GET READY, JON. GO SUIT UP.
YES MA'AM!
HERE'S YOUR WEAPON, LOADED AS ALWAYS.
A NUCLEAR WATCH, WHICH WILL TELL YOU WHAT YEAR IT IS.
AND I ADDED A PORTABLE HAND GLIDER TO YOUR SUIT.
YEAR +1
WHY?
AS I'VE SAID BEFORE, TRUST ME! I HAVE A SIXTH SENSE FOR GUESSING WHAT MIGHT COME IN HANDY ON A MISSION.

AND I'M GIVING YOU THIS. THIS IS THE GADGET YOU CAN USE TO CAPTURE THE ENTITY AND BRING IT HOME.
COOL! IT'S LIKE A...

A POKÉ BALL. I KNOW... THAT'S WHAT EVERYONE SAYS.

SON, IF I CAN GIVE YOU ONE PIECE OF ADVICE... WHEN YOU STEP OUT OF THE MACHINE, WATCH OUT FOR DINOSAURS.
DINOSAURS?
YES. EVERY TIME SOMEONE TRAVELS FAR BACK IN THE PAST, THEY ARE ATTACKED BY A DINOSAUR. AS SOON AS THEY STEP OUT OF THE MACHINE. IT'S A LAW OF PHYSICS. SO WATCH OUT!

THANKS, DAD!

ARE YOU READY, JON?
YES, MA'AM!
LET'S DO IT.

INSERT THE LIQUID LIGHT.

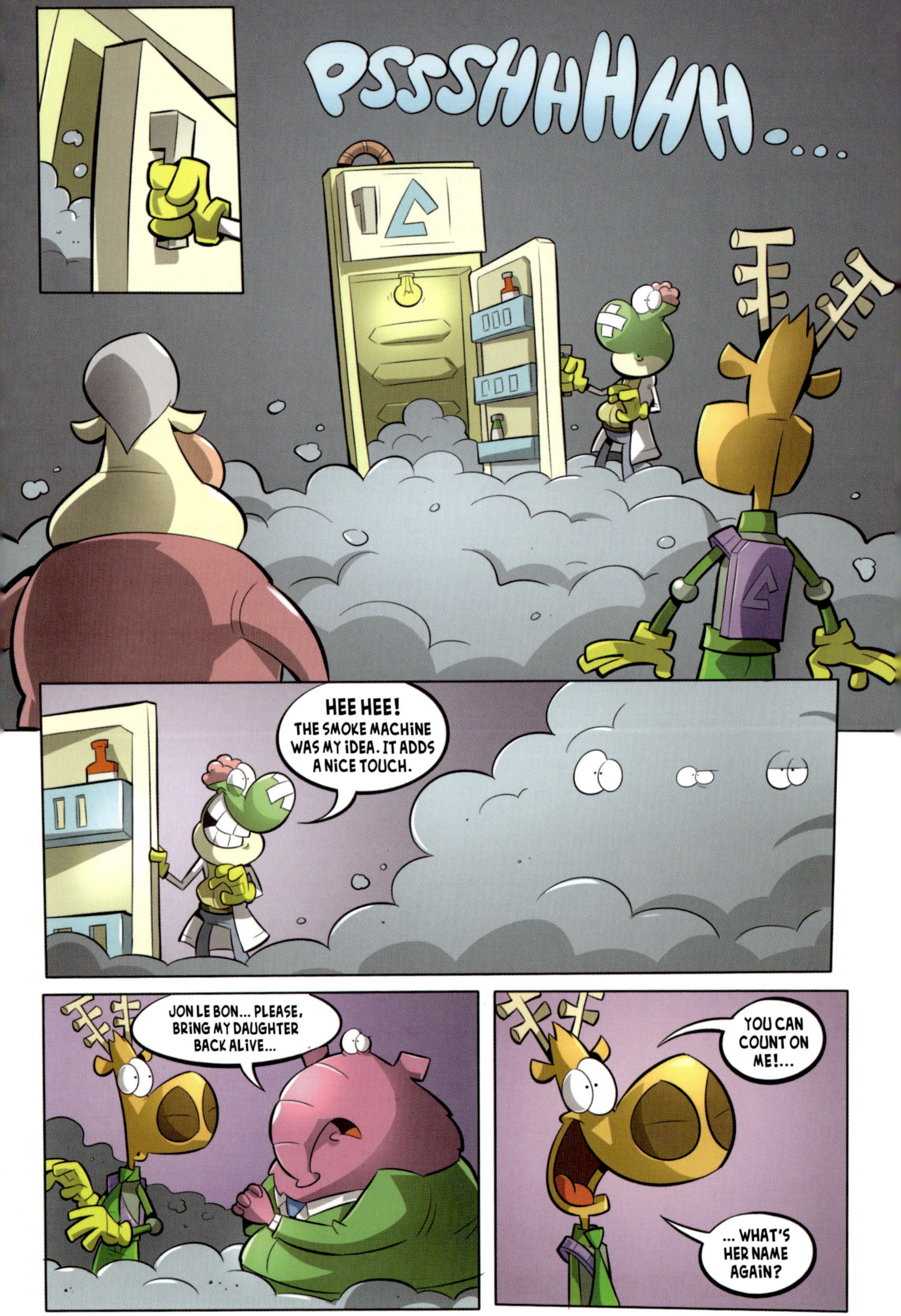

PSSSHHHHH...

HEE HEE!
THE SMOKE MACHINE WAS MY IDEA. IT ADDS A NICE TOUCH.

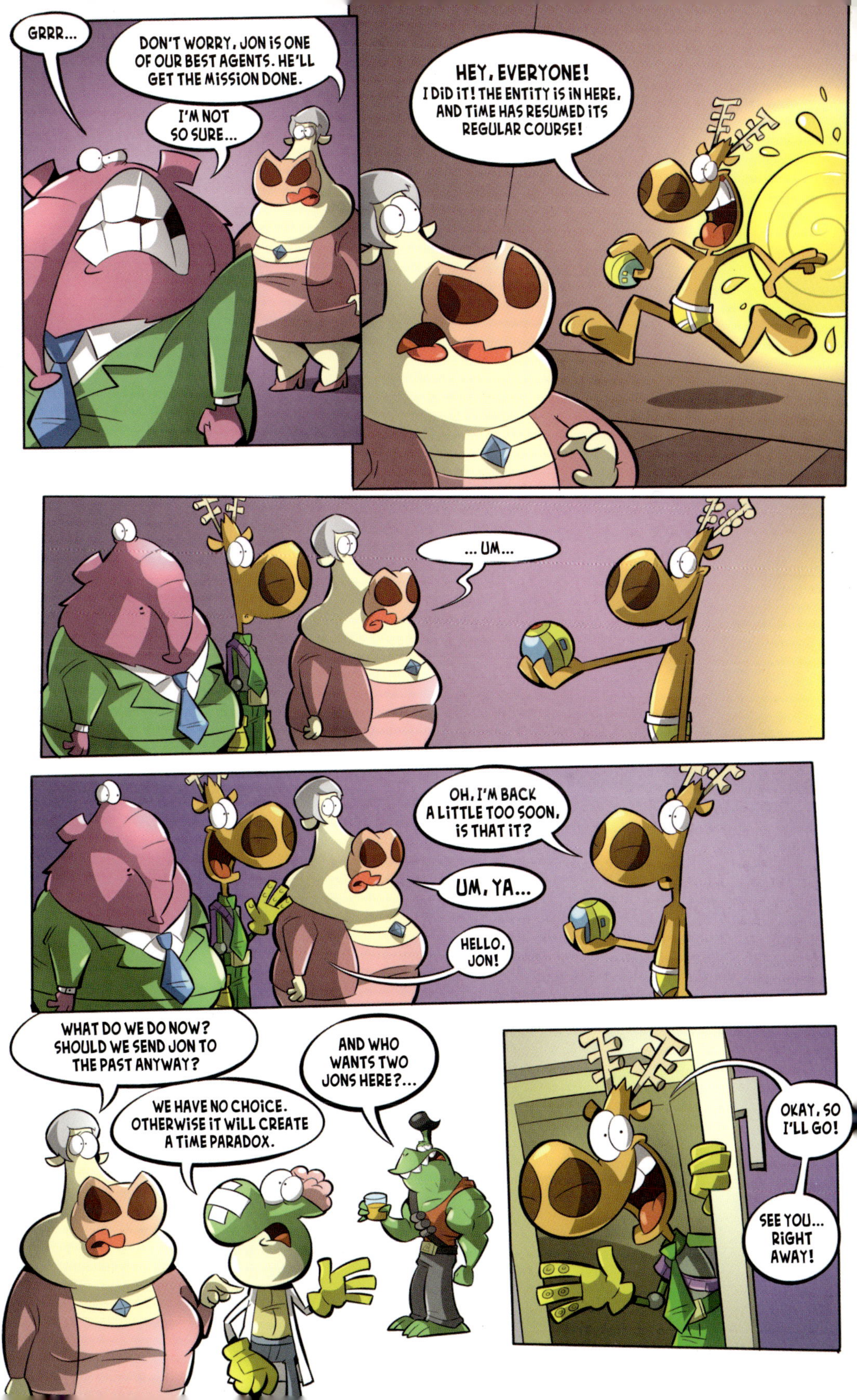

GRRR...
DON'T WORRY, JON IS ONE OF OUR BEST AGENTS. HE'LL GET THE MISSION DONE.
I'M NOT SO SURE...
HEY, EVERYONE! I DID IT! THE ENTITY IS IN HERE, AND TIME HAS RESUMED ITS REGULAR COURSE!

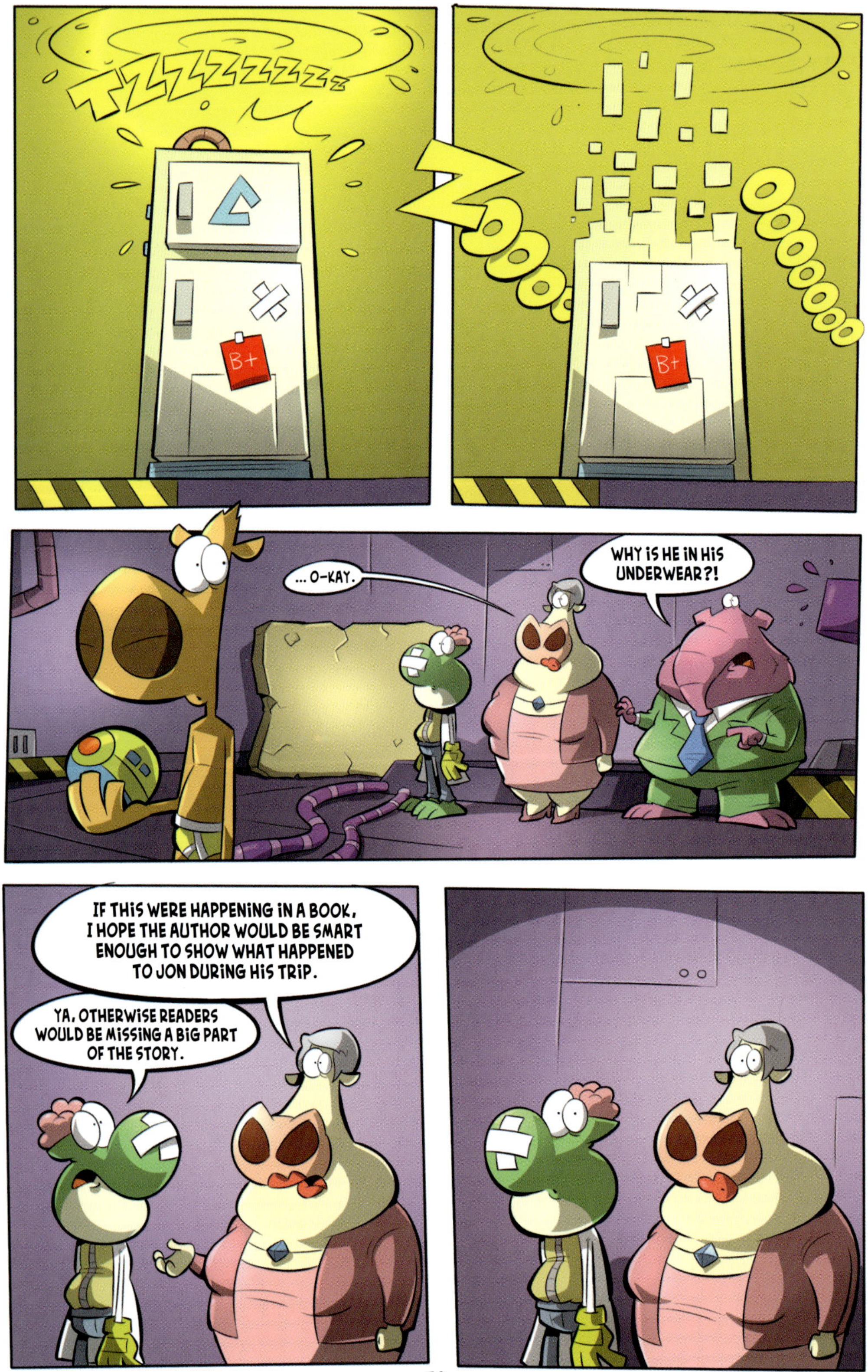

TZZZZZZZzz

ZOOOO

OOOOOOO

... O-KAY.

WHY IS HE IN HIS UNDERWEAR?!

MEANWHILE, IN THE PAST. WELL, NOT REALLY "MEANWHILE." IT'S LIKE ANOTHER TIME... IT'S GOING ON EVEN BEFORE THE BOOK STARTED SO... LET'S JUST SAY AT THE SAME TIME. UM, NO, THAT DOESN'T WORK EITHER... OKAY, YOU UNDERSTAND.
I WONDER IF CLOCKS ARE FLOATING BY AS I GO BACK IN TIME...
...COOL!

BiiiiOOOOOOO
WHOA...
IT WORKED!
AND I'VE LANDED IN THE RIGHT YEAR.
-200 000
SO, WHERE'S THE DINOSAUR...

HI THERE! WHERE DID YOU COME FROM?

UM... THE FUTURE...

OOO! THAT'S EXCITING! GUYS, THERE'S A FELLOW HERE FROM THE FUTURE!

HOW NICE!

A LITTLE LATER, BUT STILL IN THE PAST...
DINO DINO SAMBA!
THIS IS THE VILLAGE! BE SURE TO DROP BY IF YOU'RE LOOKING FOR A LITTLE EXCITEMENT! WOOHOO!
THANKS, DINOS!
VILÂJ DÈ AZUL
HELLO, EVERYONE!
THE DINOS TOLD ME YOU COULD HELP ME FIND THIS PERSON AND...
UM, WHAT ARE YOU DOING?

!

HEY, WAIT UP!

I NEED TO TALK TO YOU!

CRACK
YES!
YOU CAN'T ESCAPE! I KNOW THE RULES OF THE JURASSIC PERIOD TOO.

GIDDY UP! GIDDY UP!!!

AHHH!!!
HANG ON!
BOP
FUAT
TWIP

THANK YOU... BUT, I...
OH.

YOU OKAY?

YOU... YOU WANTED TO TALK TO ME?

OH! YES! UM...

HAVE YOU SEEN THIS GIRL?

WELL, THAT'S ALMOST IT. HE ASKED MY ORGANIZATION TO HELP HIM FIND YOU.

WHAT ORGANIZATION DO YOU WORK FOR?

SORRY, THAT'S CLASSIFIED!

EVEN 200,000 YEARS IN THE PAST?

UM, MAYBE NOT, IT'S TRUE. I'M WITH THE AGENCY.

THE AGENCY?!

YOU KNOW ABOUT IT? YOU'RE NOT SUPPOSED TO!
YES! WELL, ACTUALLY, NO ONE KNEW WHETHER IT ACTUALLY EXISTED. IT'S A BIT OF A LEGEND... BUT WOW! AN AGENT FROM THE AGENCY, I CAN'T BELIEVE IT...
IS IT TRUE THAT YOU KNOW THE SECRETS OF THE ORIGIN OF LIFE ON EARTH?
UM, I DON'T KNOW. I'M NOT A VERY HIGH RANK YET. BUT HOW ARE YOU GETTING BY IN THIS ERA? YOUR FATHER'S WORRIED ABOUT YOU...

BY POPULAR DEMAND, MY FIVE-YEAR-OLD COUSIN, JEREMY, WILL ILLUSTRATE THIS SCENE.

EVER SINCE I WAS A LITTLE GIRL, I WANTED TO FOLLOW IN MY FATHER'S FOOTSTEPS.
DADDY

HE WAS MY HERO. I FOLLOWED HIM WHEREVER HE WENT. IN THE ARMY, DURING THE WAR AND IN HIS OFFICE AS MAYOR, WHERE HE LED OUR VILLAGE.
BOOM
BOOM

WHEN I TURNED 18, HE BECAME PRESIDENT OF THE CONTINENT. I HAD NEVER BEEN SO PROUD. I THOUGHT THAT FINALLY WE WOULD HAVE A FAIR, JUST GOVERNMENT...
I WAS WRONG.

HE GAVE ME A JOB IN THE GOVERNMENT'S SECRET SERVICE. BASICALLY, I WAS A FILING CLERK. I WASN'T ALLOWED TO LOOK AT THE FILES, OF COURSE, BUT BEING CURIOUS BY NATURE...
Secret
DISAPPOINTED

I'LL ADMIT THAT SOMETIMES, I WISH I HADN'T LOOKED...
SAD
SNIFF
SECRET

FOR THE NEXT FEW WEEKS, I KEPT LOOKING THROUGH THE SECRET DOCUMENTS. IT WASN'T GETTING ANY BETTER. THE LIES, THE CORRUPTION, THE VIOLENCE... I JUST COULDN'T ACCEPT IT. I HAD TWO CHOICES: TO LEAVE THIS HORRIBLE PLACE, OR...
IDEA
Hello!

WELcome to the First MEEting of
the HETAiRiA
HETAiRiA!
YAY!
YES!

I KEPT MY JOB AT MY FATHER'S OFFICE, BUT SECRETLY I WAS PASSING INFORMATION TO A REBEL GROUP. TOGETHER WE WERE TRYING TO FOIL THE GOVERNMENT'S SECRET PLANS.
CONSPIRACY!
SEC-RET
NiAK NiAK

UNFORTUNATELY, I GOT CAUGHT.
WRA!
ANGRY
GRR...

I'VE BEEN LOCKED UP IN THE BASEMENT, NEAR THE LABS, TO WAIT FOR MY FATHER'S DECISION.
LAB

ZOP
NONO!

AND I ENDED UP HERE, AT THE EARLY DAYS OF CIVILIZATION.
WOWWW... YOU'RE AN ANARCHIST! THAT'S COOL. AND YOU'RE DOING OKAY HERE?
TOTALLY! I COULDN'T HAVE DONE BETTER. I CAN TRY TO CHANGE THE FUTURE BY TEACHING THE FOUNDATIONS OF A BETTER SOCIETY TO THE FIRST NATIONS.
AND WHAT HAPPENED WITH THE EXTRADIMENSIONAL ENTITY?
HUH? OH, I DON'T KNOW... IT WASN'T WITH ME WHEN I ARRIVED THREE MONTHS AGO. BUT I MIGHT KNOW SOMEONE WHO CAN HELP...
THE END IS NEAR! THE CORTEXES WILL SPEAK! FURNITURE WITH EYES! A GIANT ON THE MOON!
IT'S THE VILLAGE PROPHET.
SHE SEEMS NICE!
YES, WELL, I KNOW SHE LOOKS COMPLETELY BONKERS... BUT SHE CAN BE PRETTY ACCURATE IN HER PREDICTIONS!
ABOO DA BOO DA BOO

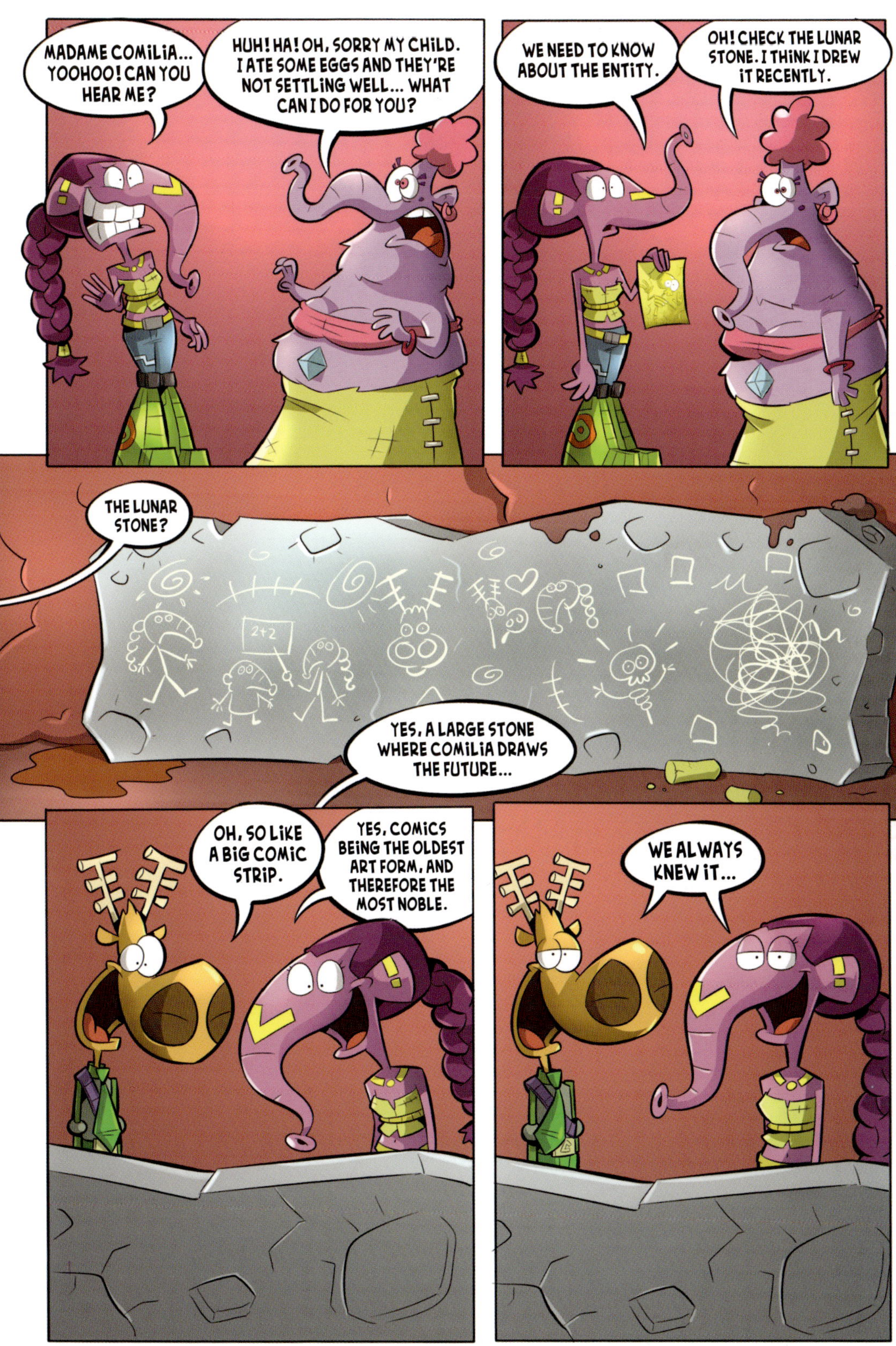
MADAME COMILIA... YOOHOO! CAN YOU HEAR ME?
HUH! HA! OH, SORRY MY CHILD. I ATE SOME EGGS AND THEY'RE NOT SETTLING WELL... WHAT CAN I DO FOR YOU?
WE NEED TO KNOW ABOUT THE ENTITY.
OH! CHECK THE LUNAR STONE. I THINK I DREW IT RECENTLY.
THE LUNAR STONE?
2+2
YES, A LARGE STONE WHERE COMILIA DRAWS THE FUTURE...
OH, SO LIKE A BIG COMIC STRIP.
YES, COMICS BEING THE OLDEST ART FORM, AND THEREFORE THE MOST NOBLE.
WE ALWAYS KNEW IT...

SO IT LOOKS LIKE THE ENTITY WILL ARRIVE IN THE NEXT FOUR DAYS. WE MUST HAVE BEEN SEPARATED BY A FEW MONTHS IN THE TIME TUNNEL.
WOULD YOU CONSIDER STAYING IN THE VILLAGE IN THE MEANTIME?
I CAN'T! THEY'RE EXPECTING ME BACK AT THE AGENCY.

JON... THEY'RE NOT EVEN BORN YET.

HA! OF COURSE! SO I'LL STAY WITH YOU!
... COOL!

HEY, MADAME COMILIA. YOUR DRAWINGS GET A LITTLE HAZY TOWARD THE END... DO YOU KNOW WHAT'S GOING TO HAPPEN?

THE RODENT DUPLICATE ITSELF IN A LABORATORY STAG, THE FATHER IS AUTOMATION, BIG COMPANY IS GENESIS OF THE BIG TEETH, AND HIS POWER COME FROM THE LIGHT BULB!
ABOO DABOO DABOO!!!
OKAY, WE'RE GOING NOW...
AH! I THINK I UNDERSTOOD THAT TIME!
DAY 1.
COME ON, JON. I'LL INTRODUCE YOU TO THE AZULS.
IT'S THE DEMON IN A TIE!
HAVE MERCY, SPARE MY BROTHERS!
HELLO!
UM, WHENEVER THEY'RE INTIMIDATED BY SOMEONE OR SOMETHING, THEY THINK THEY'RE GODS OR DEMONS...

OH, CREATURE FROM THE HEAVENS, SHOW ME HOW TO FLY!

I SALUTE YOU, CLOUD GOD!

I AM AT YOUR SERVICE, TREE TRUNK DIVINITY!

GREAT!
AHHH!

OKAY, OKAY, JON'S NOT A GOD. HE'S FROM THE FUTURE, LIKE ME.
THE FUTURE?! OH! DID YOU EVER FIND THE RUINS OF OUR ANCIENT CITIES?

THOSE ARE YOUR CITIES? THERE'S NOT MUCH TO THEM...
YES, WELL ACTUALLY, WE BUILD RUINS THAT LOOK LIKE THEY WERE VERY LARGE CITIES. THAT WAY, PEOPLE IN THE FUTURE WILL WONDER HOW WE COULD HAVE DONE IT IN SPITE OF OUR PRIMITIVE TOOLS.
SO DID IT WORK?

UM... YES!
SO COOL!

OTHER THAN THAT, WHAT DO YOU DO TO PASS THE TIME?
OH, THE USUAL CAVEMAN THINGS. SMASHING ROCKS TOGETHER FOR FIRE, INVENTING THE WHEEL, DYING AT AGE TWENTY-EIGHT...
OH AND WE USED TO SWIM NAKED TOO, BUT MAPLE TAUGHT US THAT IT WAS BAD...
I DID NOT... IT'S JUST THAT I FELT UNCOMFORTABLE SEEING THEM NAKED ALL THE TIME.
JON?
FOLLOW ME, EVERYONE. WE'RE GOING SWIMMING!!
YA!!!
DAY 2
THERE'S ONE RIGHT THERE...

DO YOU EAT THOSE CREATURES? BUT THEY'RE SO CUTE!
NO, NO, MAPLE ALSO TAUGHT US THE PLEASURES OF VEGETARIANISM.
YA, PLEASURES.
SO WE DO OTHER STUFF WITH THOSE CREATURES...

CHOP THE VEGETABLES, COOK THE POTATOES! AREN'T YOU GETTING SICK OF IT?
DO LIKE I DO. SPIT IN THEIR SOUP.

WHAT? YOU ENSLAVE BUNNIES!? BUT I TOLD YOU...
COME ON! NO MEAT, NO SLAVERY. WHAT DO WE HAVE LEFT?

... MAY THUNDER COME CRASHING DOWN ON YOU...
AHHH! FORGIVE ME, GOD LADY!!
FORGIVE ME...

PAF

I THOUGHT I TOLD YOU NOT TO SET FOOT ON AMARILLOS LAND!
GULP!
THAT'S AN ACT OF WAR!
LET'S BUST SOME HEADS!!!
NO! NO! NO!
YOU'RE NOT GOING TO FIGHT AGAIN WITH YOUR SO-CALLED "ENEMY TRIBE"?!

OH, COME ON, MAPLE! JUST FIFTEEN MINUTES! IT'S THE STONE AGE. THERE'S NOTHING ELSE TO DO...
HE'S RIGHT. WE DON'T HAVE VIDEO GAMES... SO WHY NOT FIGHT FOR REAL?
OH, OKAY. BUT NOT FOR TOO LONG.
YAY!

DAY 3.
OKAY, EVERYONE. NOW I'M GOING TO EXPLAIN HOW RAIN WORKS.
I KNOW! IT'S THE GODS PEEING.
NO, FOR THE LAST TIME, THAT'S NOT IT!!
2+2=4

SO IT ALL STARTS WHEN WATER VAPOUR EVAPORATED BY THE SUN CONDENSATES IN THE CLOUD THROUGH COOLING...

WOULD YOU PLEASE TAKE YOUR FOOT OUT OF YOUR MOUTH?!?

SHORRY, MA'AM...

SIGH
OKAY, SO YOU'RE GOING TO DO YOUR ORAL PRESENTATION NOW. I HOPE YOU'RE PREPARED.
YES! YES!...
2+2=4

2+2=4
HELLO, UM... I... THE... UM...

COME ON. WHAT ARE YOU WAITING FOR?
I'M SHY!

I KNOW HOW YOU FEEL. MR. SHORTHAND GAVE ME A TIP FOR THAT A LONG TIME AGO. IMAGINE EVERYONE HERE IN THEIR UNDERWEAR.

BUT EVERYONE IS ALREADY IN THEIR UNDERWEAR.
HEY! THAT'S TRUE! YOU TOO, COME TO THINK OF IT.
OH, NO! IT'S A NIGHTMARE!!!

ARRRRRRRH
CLASS IS OVER. YOU CAN GO BACK TO HAVING FUN.
AND THIS IS WHY, IN TRIBAL MEETINGS, IT IS IMPORTANT TO SPEED UP THE DEMOCRATIC PROCESS AND...
WHO'S HE? I DIDN'T NOTICE HIM BEFORE.
OH, HIM.. THAT'S HORRIDILUS, OUR "PRESIDENT."
WOW! THEY'RE EVOLVING QUICKLY!
YA... I'M TRYING TO INTRODUCE A DEMOCRATIC SYSTEM IN THE VILLAGE. BUT IT'S NOT EASY GIVEN HOW IGNORANT EVERYONE IS...

AND WHAT WITH THE MAINTENANCE WORK IN THE KITCHEN, WE HAVE NO CHOICE BUT TO REDUCE THE NUMBER OF PINK RABBITS TO BALANCE THE BUDGET, AND...
WHAT?! LESS FOOD! WHAT'S HE SAYING?!?
HEY, FOUR EYES! EAT THIS!

OW!

HEY, THAT LOOKS LIKE A FUN GAME!
LET'S CALL IT... THROW ROCKS AT PEOPLE'S FACES!
YA!

WOW! IT'S ALMOST LIKE OUR ERA!

DAY 4 – A FEW HOURS BEFORE THE ENTITY'S ARRIVAL...
TELL US ABOUT THE FUTURE AGAIN, JON.
YA!!!

OKAY, UM... IT'S NOT ONLY ELEPHANTS AND GIRAFFES THAT WALK ON TWO LEGS, BUT ALL THE ANIMALS. EVEN DEER, LIKE ME!

WHAT? YOU'RE A DEER? I COULD HAVE SWORN YOU WERE A REINDEER.
I WOULD HAVE SAID A MOOSE.
A MOOSE? HAVE YOU ACTUALLY SEEN ONE? THEY'RE WAY BIGGER THAN HIM!

OH! I THOUGHT HE WAS A DOG.
BUT HE HAS ANTLERS, STUPID!
THEY DON'T LOOK LIKE ANTLERS...

ANYWAY, DOGS DON'T HAVE NOSTRILS LIKE THAT.
DEERS DON'T EITHER, I'LL HAVE YOU KNOW.

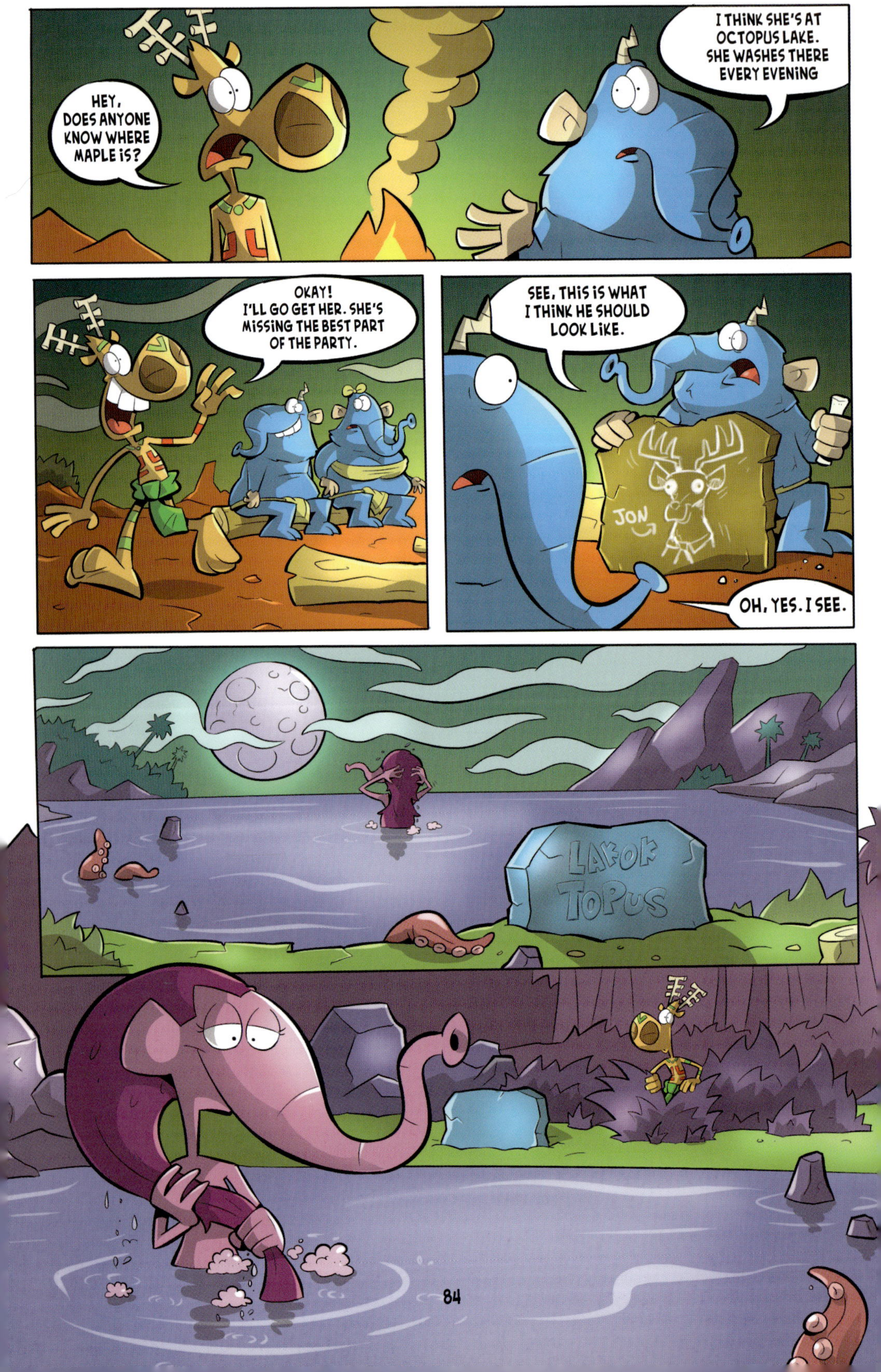

HEY, DOES ANYONE KNOW WHERE MAPLE IS?
I THINK SHE'S AT OCTOPUS LAKE. SHE WASHES THERE EVERY EVENING

OKAY! I'LL GO GET HER. SHE'S MISSING THE BEST PART OF THE PARTY.

SEE, THIS IS WHAT I THINK HE SHOULD LOOK LIKE.
JON
OH, YES. I SEE.

MAPLE! WHAT ARE YOU DOING HERE? YOU'RE MISSING THE PARTY!
HI, JON! I WAS FRESHENING UP A LITTLE... DO YOU WANT TO COME WITH ME?
YES!... ABSOLUTELY...
CANNONBALL!!!
HEE HEE. NICE ONE!

SO, HOW DO YOU LIKE IT HERE?

IT'S GREAT. I REALLY LIKE YOUR FRIENDS. WHAT ABOUT YOU? ARE YOU ENJOYING YOURSELF?

YES, QUITE A BIT.
I ALMOST PREFER THIS ERA TO OURS. EVERYTHING IS SO MUCH SIMPLER.

DID YOU KNOW THAT YOUR EYES LOOK LOVELY IN THE MOONLIGHT?

OH YA? YOU KNOW, I FIND THEM...
WEIRD!
HAVE YOU NOTICED THAT ONE OF THEM IS BIGGER THAN THE OTHER? AND CHECK THIS OUT...

IF I TURN MY HEAD, THEY CHANGE SIDES!
IT JUST DOESN'T MAKE SENSE!

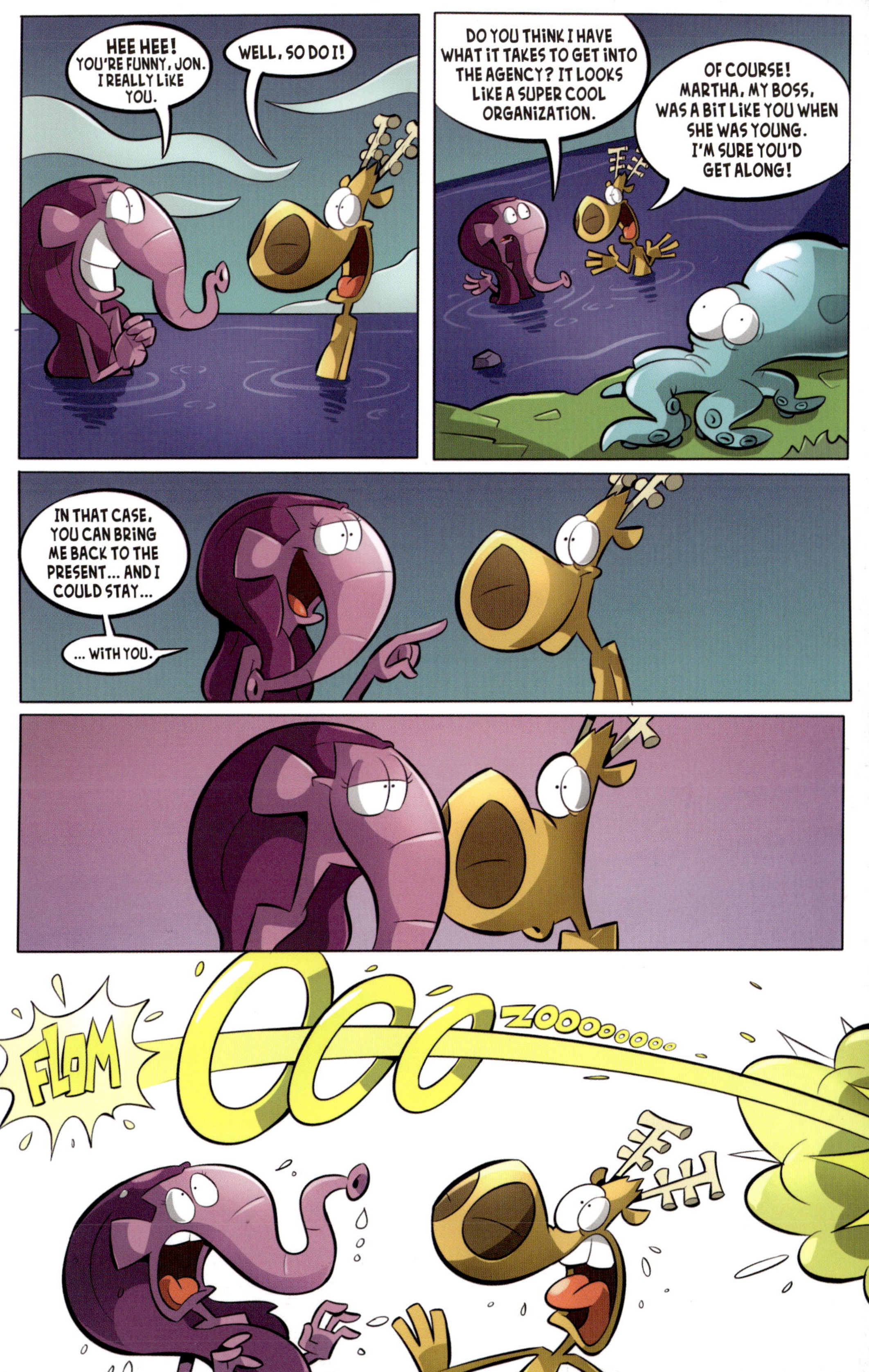
HEE HEE! YOU'RE FUNNY, JON. I REALLY LIKE YOU.
WELL, SO DO I!
DO YOU THINK I HAVE WHAT IT TAKES TO GET INTO THE AGENCY? IT LOOKS LIKE A SUPER COOL ORGANIZATION.
OF COURSE! MARTHA, MY BOSS, WAS A BIT LIKE YOU WHEN SHE WAS YOUNG. I'M SURE YOU'D GET ALONG!
IN THAT CASE, YOU CAN BRING ME BACK TO THE PRESENT... AND I COULD STAY...
... WITH YOU.
FLOM
ZOOOOOOOOO

I THINK THAT
WAS THE ENTITY.
IT'S HERE.

THE AZULS!
THEY SHOULDN'T GET
SO CLOSE!

IT MUST BE A
GIFT FROM THE
GODS!
... OR THEY JUST
FLUSHED...

OH!
IT'S PRETTY!

STEP BACK!!!
IT'S GOING TO BLOW
YOU UP!!!

AHHH!!!
PANIC!
PANIC!

ZZZZZZ

HEY! I JUST DISCOVERED THAT BEING BURNT REALLY HURTS!
SUPER! ARRGHHH!!!

JON! DO YOU HAVE THE BALL WITH YOU?!
IT'S IN MY HUT!!

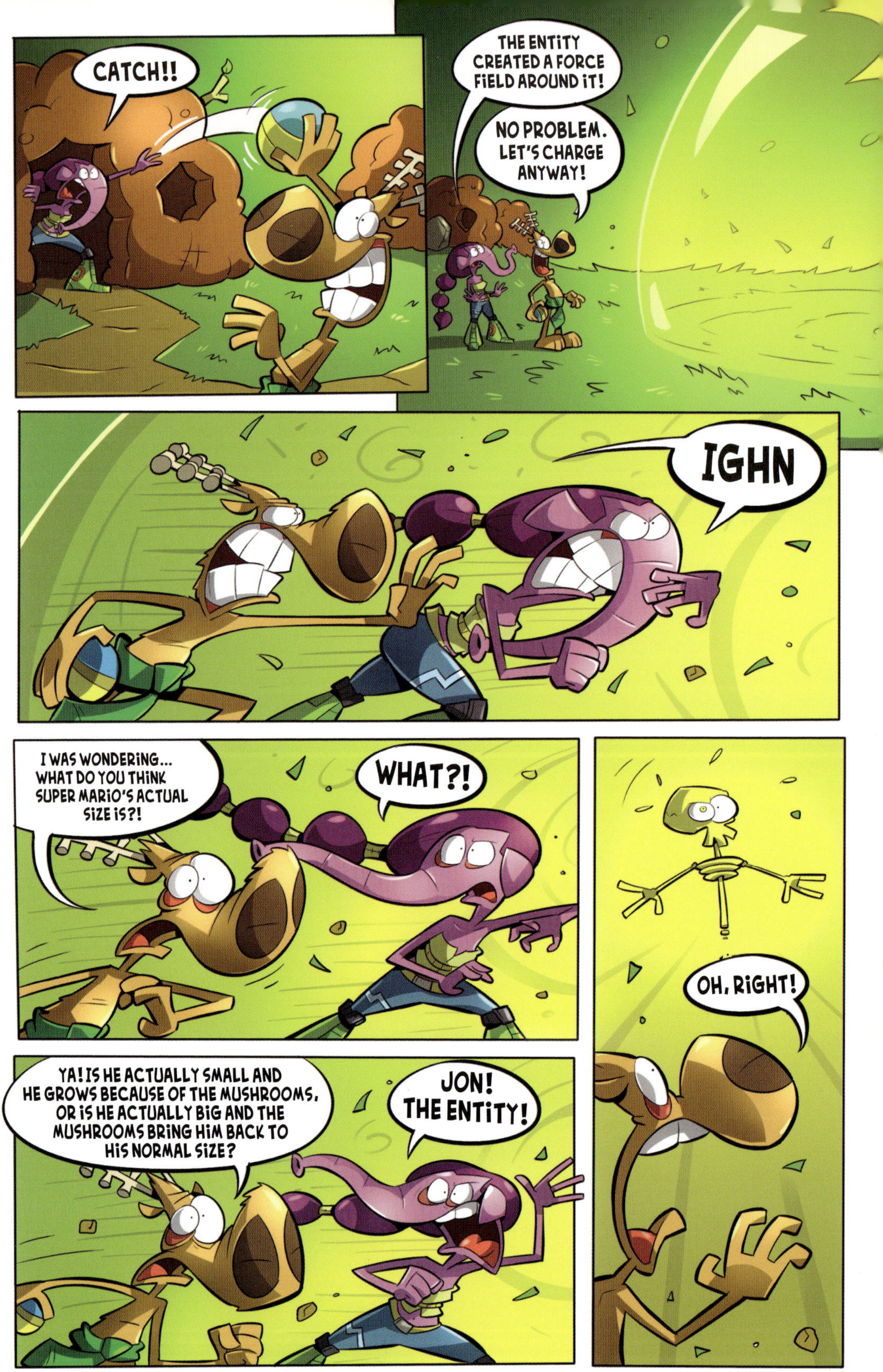

CATCH!!

THE ENTITY CREATED A FORCE FIELD AROUND IT!

NO PROBLEM. LET'S CHARGE ANYWAY!

IGHN

HELLO!
WOULD YOU LIKE
TO POP IN HERE?
BABOOM

ARGH... MY HEAD...
MORNING! COFFEE?
DO YOU EVER FEEL BAD?
NOT AFTER SUCH A GOOD NIGHT'S SLEEP!
!
LIKE YOU SAID... IT WAS A VERY GOOD NIGHT!

WE SLEPT FOR A WHOLE YEAR! NO WONDER I FEEL SO RESTED!
-199
999

NO, JON! THE ENTITY'S SHOCKWAVE MUST HAVE BLOWN US ONE YEAR INTO THE FUTURE!
OOOOOOW. SO FAR THIS MISSION HAS BEEN VERY BIZARRE.

COME ON. LET'S GO SEE WHAT HAPPENED.

MINE

GOODNESS, THEY EVOLVED QUICKLY WITH YOUR ADVICE.
I DON'T THINK THIS HAD ANYTHING TO DO WITH ME...
AAAHHHRRR!!
GOD I HATE MY LIFE...
THE SHIFT IS OVER, EVERYONE. LET'S GO HOME.
YAY...
HEY GUYS! WHAT ARE YOU DOING? WHAT HAPPENED?
MAPLE! JON! WE HAVEN'T SEEN YOU IN FOREVER!!
SORRY, WE SLEPT A LONG TIME...
NO NO, WE WERE CAUGHT IN A TIME SHOCK. BUT TELL ME, WHAT HAPPENED HERE?

OH, THIS IS WHAT HAPPENED WHEN THE GRAND HORRIDILUS TOOK OVER!
DO YOU REMEMBER THE PRESIDENT? WELL, WHEN THE LITTLE YELLOW MAN CAME DOWN TO EARTH, HE GAVE HIM ALL OF HIS POWERS. SINCE THEN, HE'S FORCED US TO WORK IN THE MINE TO AMASS RICHES FOR HIM.
THAT'S ABSURD, HE DOESN'T NEED ALL THIS.
NO, BUT IT'S PRETTY.
BUT IT'S NOT SO BAD. IN EXCHANGE FOR OUR WORK, HE GIVES US ROOM AND BOARD AND FREE LUDO-LEPUS MATCHES!
GO ON! BUST HIS HEAD!
OOO! I'LL BET ON THE ONE WITH THE BIG TEETH!
OKAY!

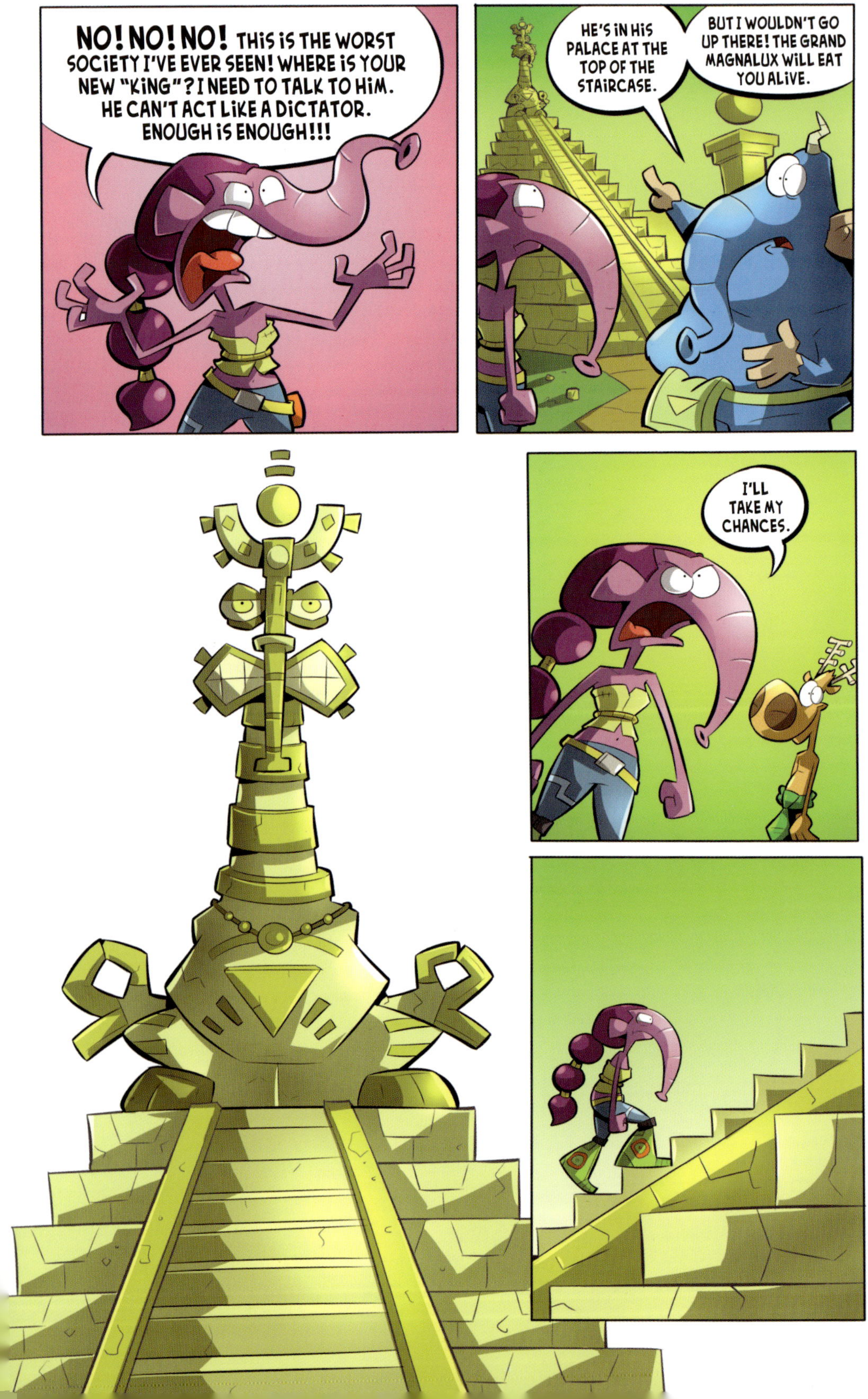

I'LL TAKE MY CHANCES.

YOU ARE NOT AUTHORIZED TO PASS, MISERABLE VERMIN.
HELLO, MAGNALUX. I'M JON.
HELLO.
WELL, WE'RE GOING IN ANYWAY, YOU BIG... BIG UGLY STATUE!!
AS INSULTS GO, THAT WASN'T THE BEST...
I KNOW. I CAN NEVER COME UP WITH GOOD COMEBACKS WHEN I'M MAD...
TO SEE THE EMPEROR, YOU NEED TO ANSWER... THE ANSWERLESS RIDDLE.
UM, ACTUALLY... IS IT A KING OR AN EMPEROR?
GO AHEAD.
WHAT HAS FOUR LEGS IN THE MORNING, FOUR LEGS AT NOON AND FOUR LEGS IN THE EVENING?

... A CHAIR?
UM...
WELL, UM...
THAT'S RIGHT.
LET'S MAKE IT
TWO OUT OF
THREE.

... IF YOU
LIKE...

GREAT.
WHAT HAPPENS
WHEN AN UNSTOPPABLE
FORCE MEETS AN
IMMOVABLE OBJECT?

... WELL NOTHING.

... YES, CORRECT
ANSWER...
ONE
MORE?

...

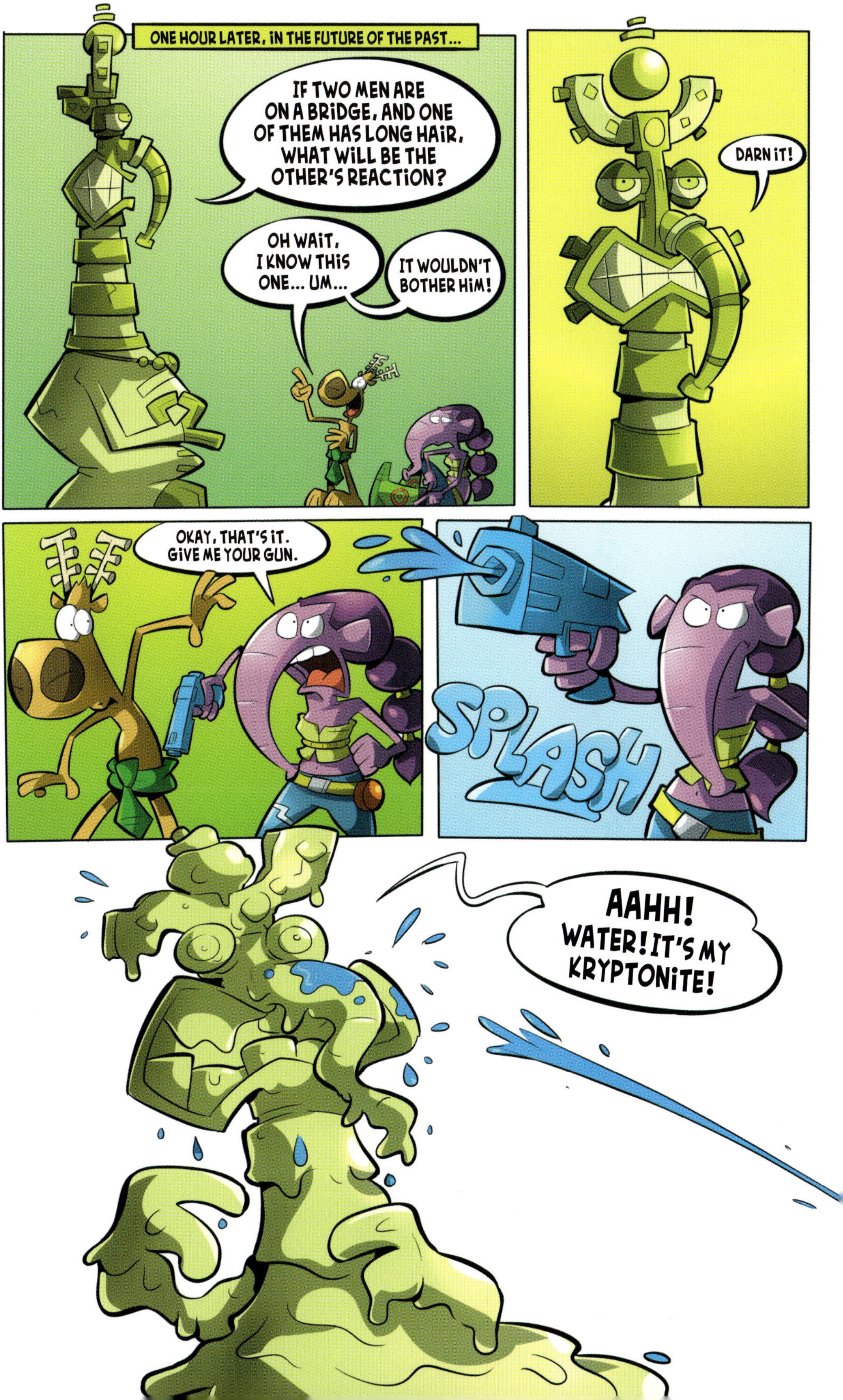

ONE HOUR LATER, IN THE FUTURE OF THE PAST...

IF TWO MEN ARE ON A BRIDGE, AND ONE OF THEM HAS LONG HAIR, WHAT WILL BE THE OTHER'S REACTION?

OH WAIT, I KNOW THIS ONE... UM...

IT WOULDN'T BOTHER HIM!

OKAY, THAT'S IT. GIVE ME YOUR GUN.

SPLASH

AAHH! WATER! IT'S MY KRYPTONITE!

YOUR GUN IS A WATER GUN?!
WOW. THAT WAS EASY.
I'VE HAD IT SINCE I WAS LITTLE, AND IT'S ALWAYS WORKED. SEE?!
ABLURG...
HEY! MAGNALUX WAS MADE OF PLASTER!
IF ONLY WE HAD KNOWN...
COME ON EVERYONE. LET'S PUT AN END TO YOUR MAD DICTATOR'S TERROR REGIME!

WHERE ARE YOU HIDING, YOU, YOU... MEANIE!
YOU SHOULD REALLY GIVE UP ON THE INSULTS...
MWAHAH AHAHA!!! TREMBLE BEFORE THE LORD HORRIDILUS!!!
BUT I THOUGHT HE WAS AN EMPEROR!
HA! YOU SEE! HE'S TOO POWERFUL FOR US!!
JON, CAN I BORROW YOUR GUN AGAIN?
KNOCK YOURSELF OUT.

AH! MY HAIRDO!

PAK
CLOK
TANG
BEDANG

SO... CARE TO EXPLAIN?

WELL, UM... I...

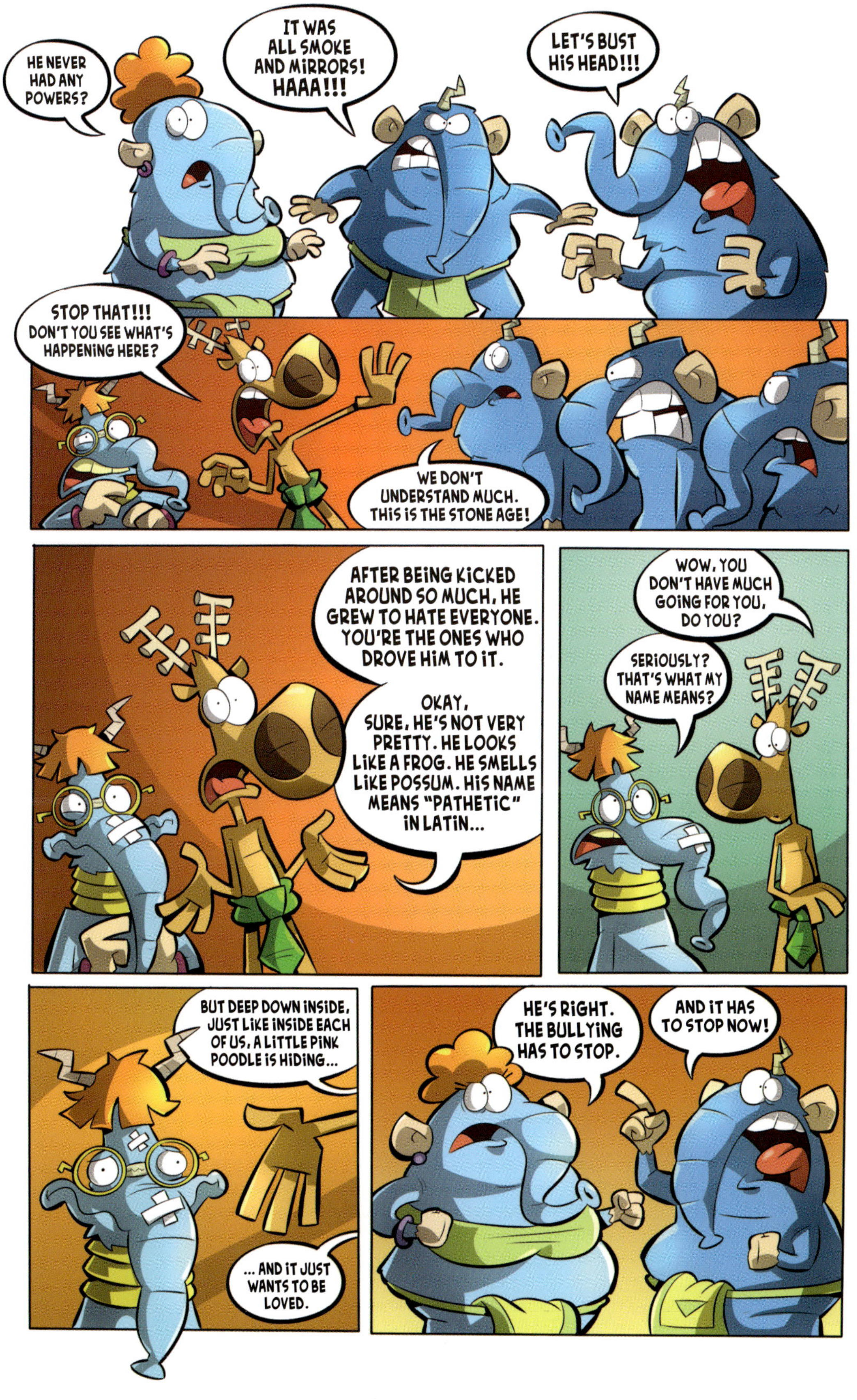

HE NEVER HAD ANY POWERS?
IT WAS ALL SMOKE AND MIRRORS! HAAA!!!
LET'S BUST HIS HEAD!!!

STOP THAT!!! DON'T YOU SEE WHAT'S HAPPENING HERE?
WE DON'T UNDERSTAND MUCH. THIS IS THE STONE AGE!

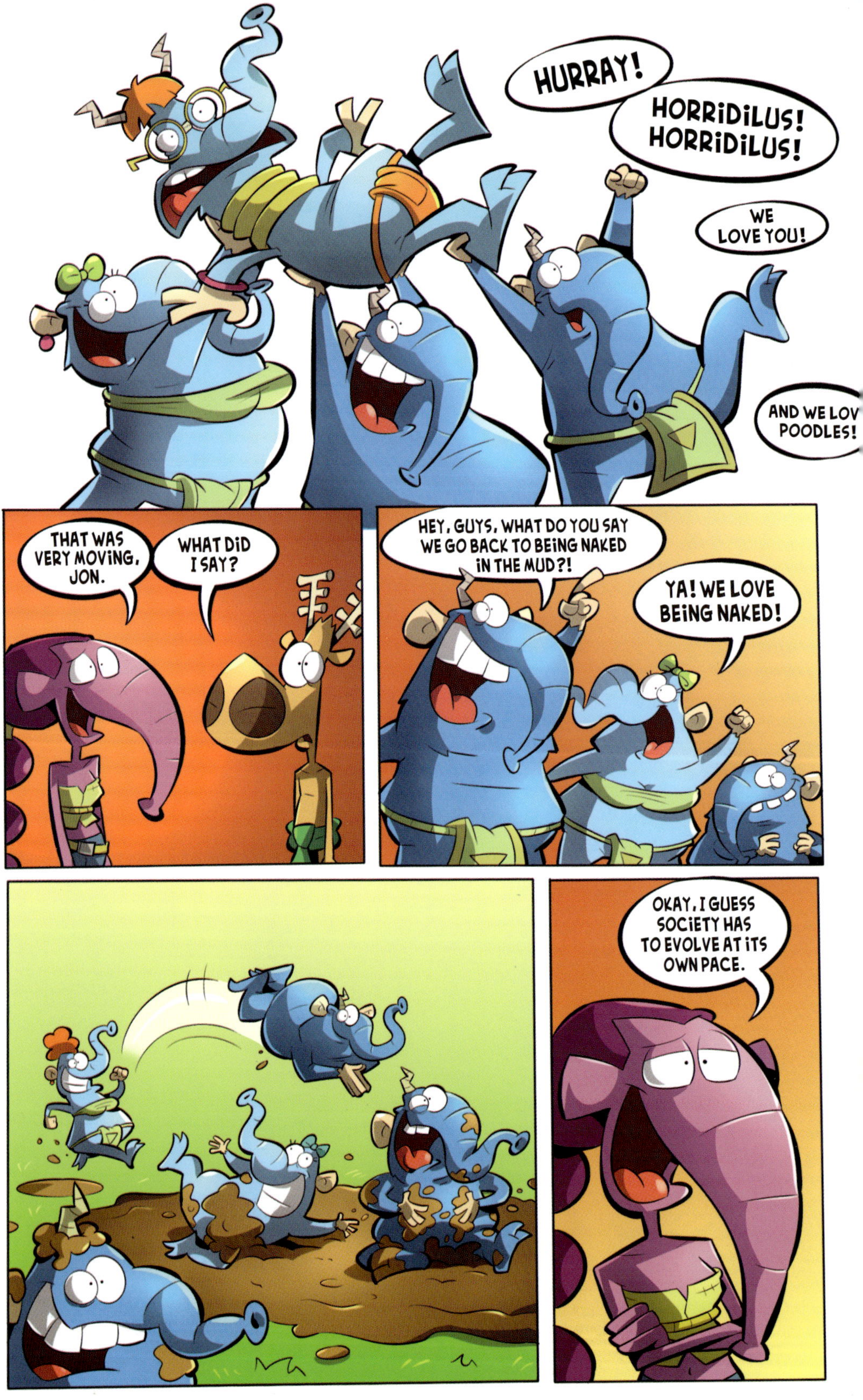

HURRAY!
HORRIDILUS! HORRIDILUS!
WE LOVE YOU!
AND WE LOV POODLES!

THAT WAS VERY MOVING, JON.
WHAT DID I SAY?

HEY, GUYS, WHAT DO YOU SAY WE GO BACK TO BEING NAKED IN THE MUD?!
YA! WE LOVE BEING NAKED!

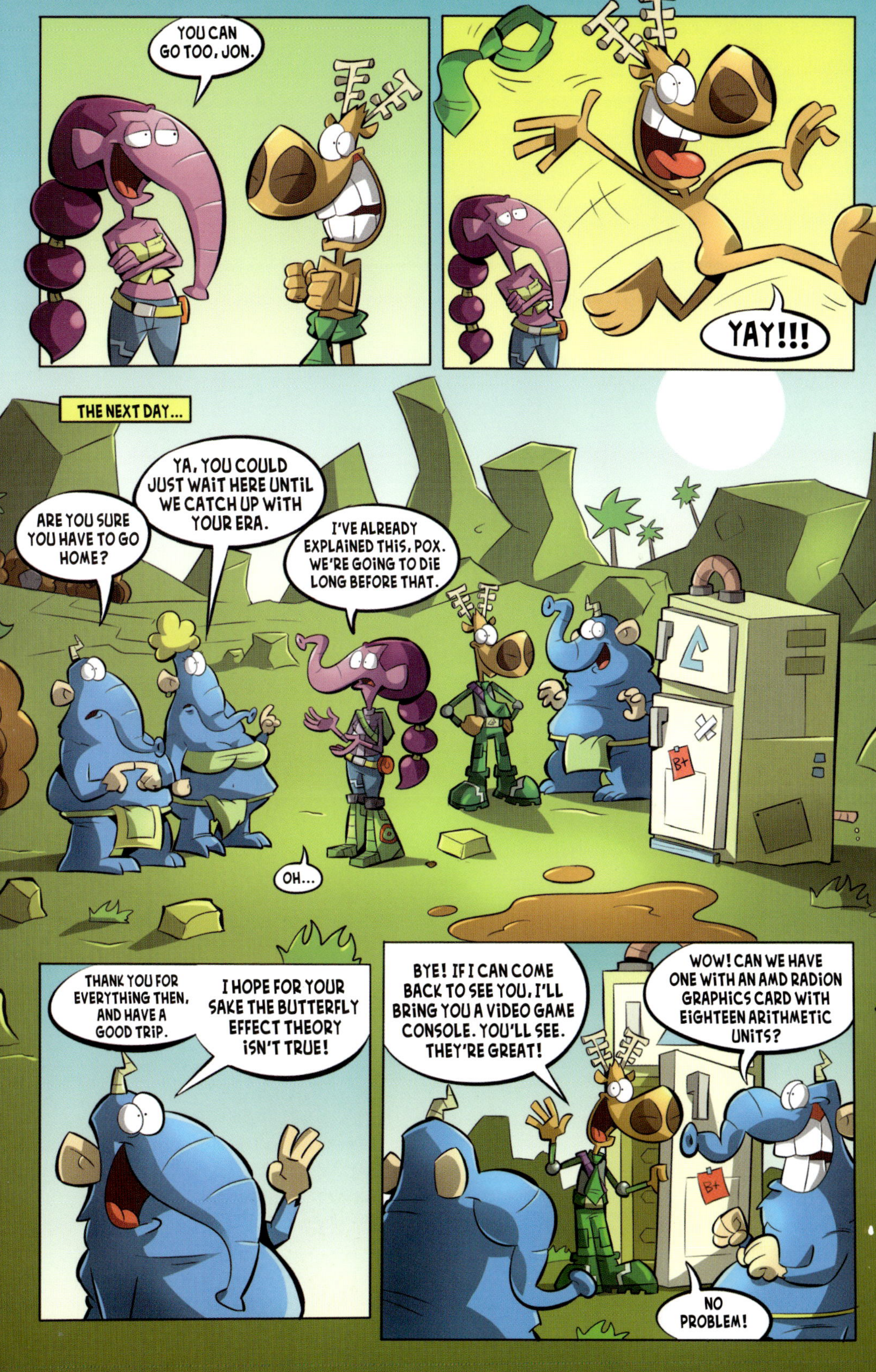
YOU CAN GO TOO, JON.
YAY!!!
THE NEXT DAY...
ARE YOU SURE YOU HAVE TO GO HOME?
YA, YOU COULD JUST WAIT HERE UNTIL WE CATCH UP WITH YOUR ERA.
I'VE ALREADY EXPLAINED THIS, POX. WE'RE GOING TO DIE LONG BEFORE THAT.
OH...
THANK YOU FOR EVERYTHING THEN, AND HAVE A GOOD TRIP.
I HOPE FOR YOUR SAKE THE BUTTERFLY EFFECT THEORY ISN'T TRUE!
BYE! IF I CAN COME BACK TO SEE YOU, I'LL BRING YOU A VIDEO GAME CONSOLE. YOU'LL SEE. THEY'RE GREAT!
WOW! CAN WE HAVE ONE WITH AN AMD RADION GRAPHICS CARD WITH EIGHTEEN ARITHMETIC UNITS?
NO PROBLEM!

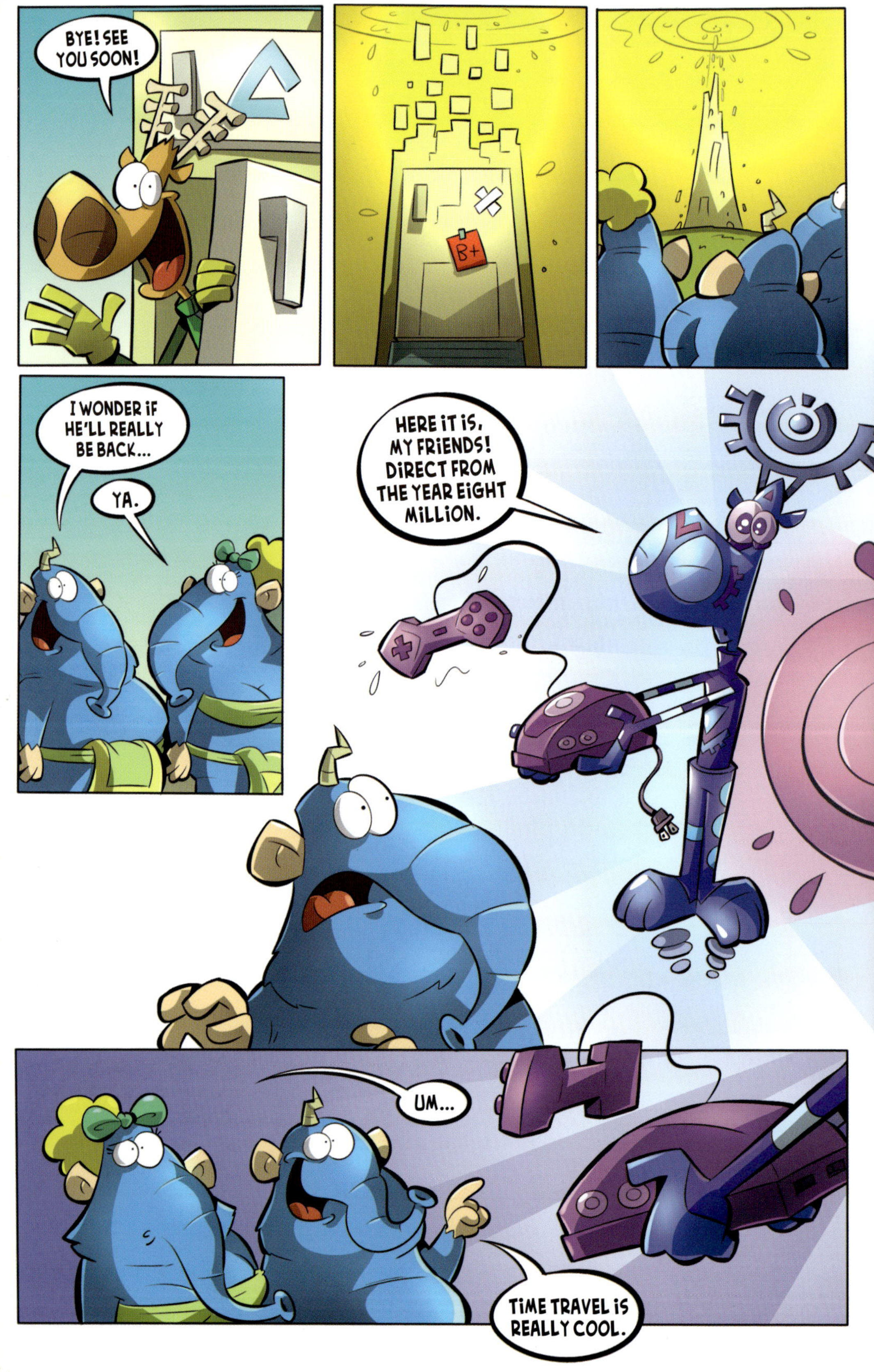
BYE! SEE YOU SOON!
B+
I WONDER IF HE'LL REALLY BE BACK...
YA.
HERE IT IS, MY FRIENDS! DIRECT FROM THE YEAR EIGHT MILLION.
UM...
TIME TRAVEL IS REALLY COOL.

WHAT AN ADVENTURE. READY TO FACE YOUR FATHER?
IT'S NOW OR NEVER.
B+
HEY, COME TO THINK OF IT, WE COMPLETELY FORGOT TO CAPTURE THE ENTITY IN THE END!
AHHHH! STOP THE MACHINE!!!
B+
OH NO.
B+

THE PRESENT...

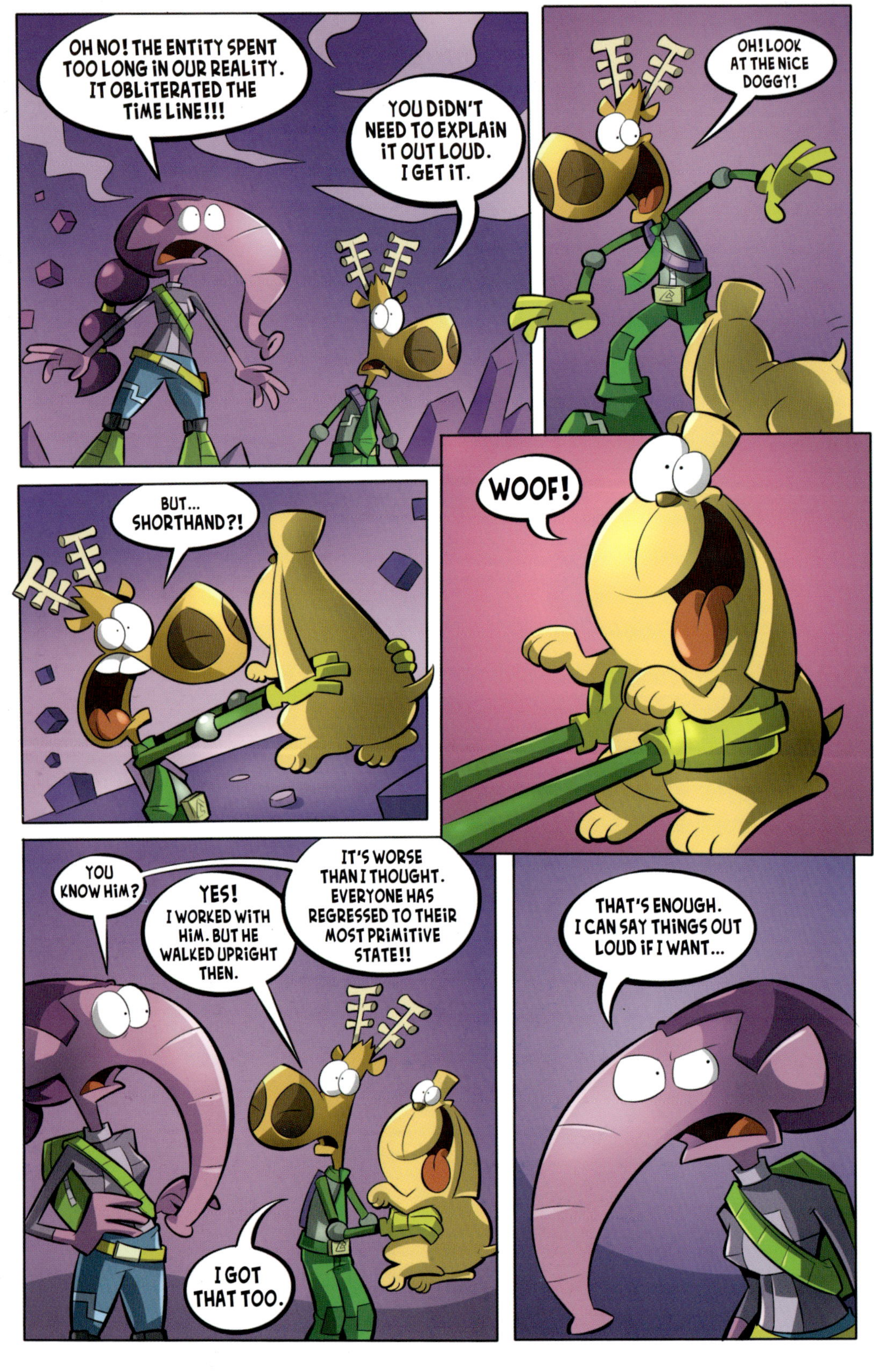
OH NO! THE ENTITY SPENT TOO LONG IN OUR REALITY. IT OBLITERATED THE TIME LINE!!!
YOU DIDN'T NEED TO EXPLAIN IT OUT LOUD. I GET IT.
OH! LOOK AT THE NICE DOGGY!
BUT... SHORTHAND?!
WOOF!
YOU KNOW HIM?
YES! I WORKED WITH HIM. BUT HE WALKED UPRIGHT THEN.
IT'S WORSE THAN I THOUGHT. EVERYONE HAS REGRESSED TO THEIR MOST PRIMITIVE STATE!!
I GOT THAT TOO.
THAT'S ENOUGH. I CAN SAY THINGS OUT LOUD IF I WANT...

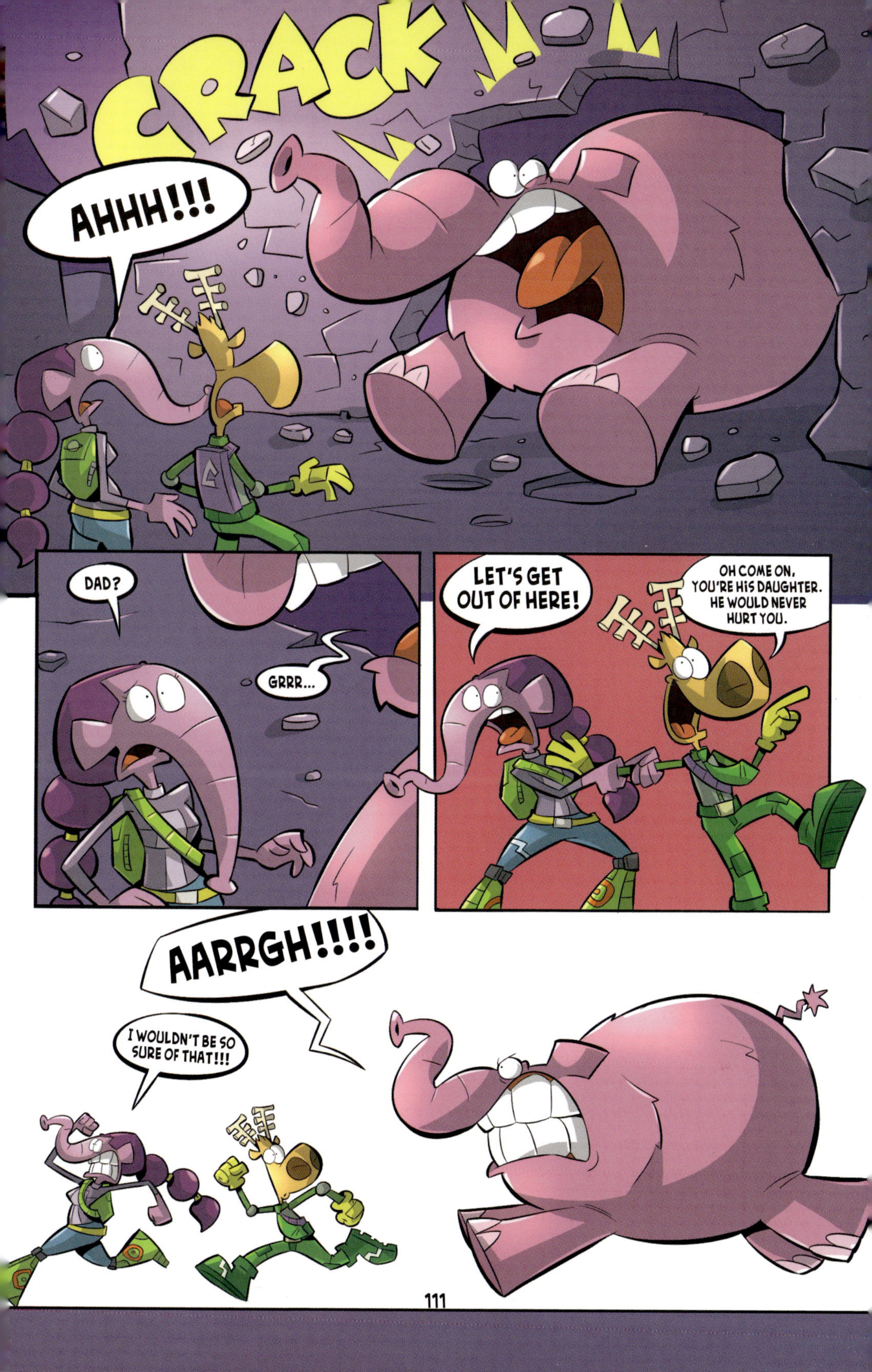
CRACK
AHHH!!!
DAD?
GRRR...
LET'S GET OUT OF HERE!
OH COME ON, YOU'RE HIS DAUGHTER. HE WOULD NEVER HURT YOU.
AARRGH!!!!
I WOULDN'T BE SO SURE OF THAT!!!

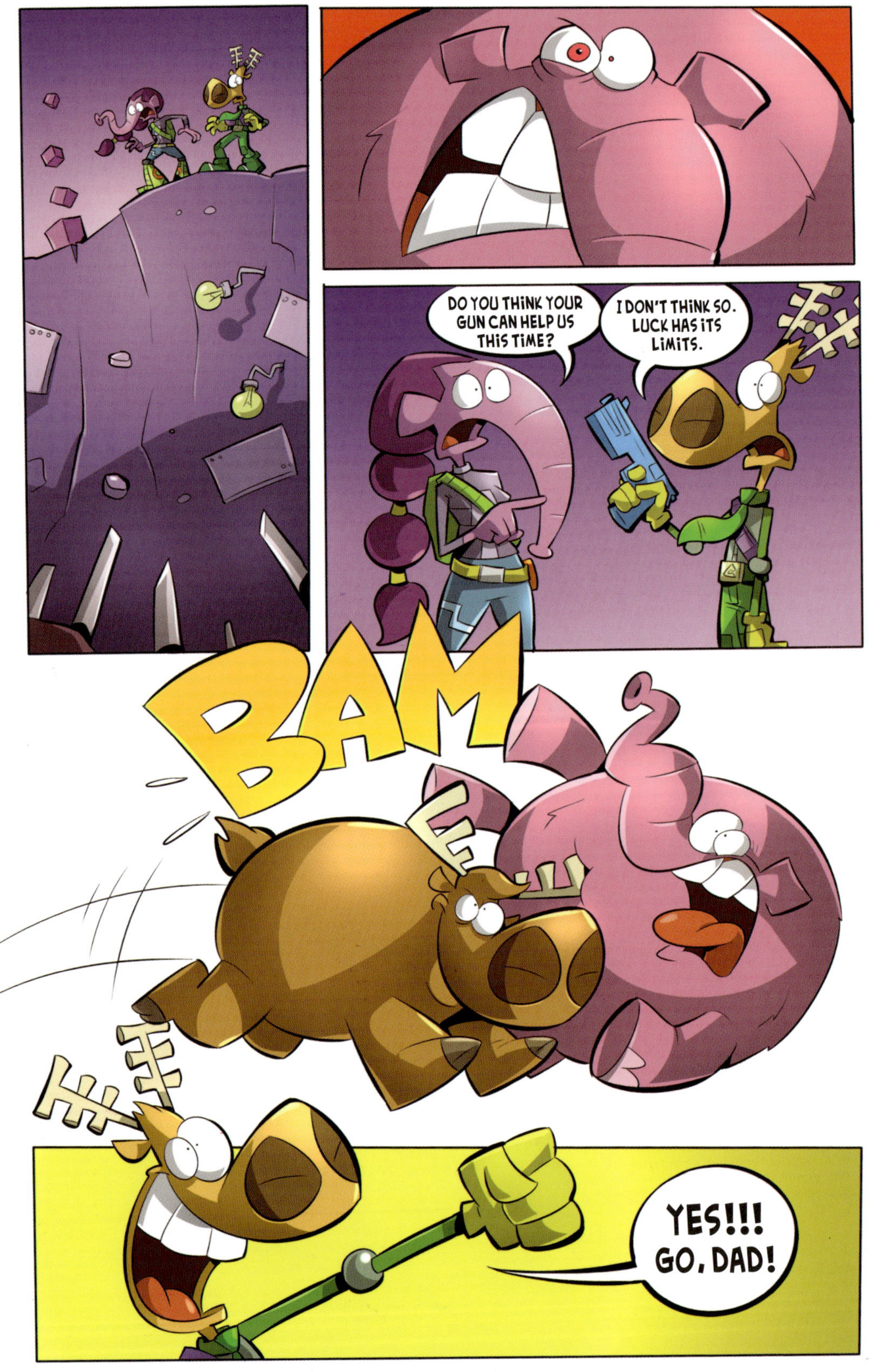
DO YOU THINK YOUR GUN CAN HELP US THIS TIME?
I DON'T THINK SO. LUCK HAS ITS LIMITS.
BAM
YES!!! GO, DAD!

STOK
THANKS, JON'S DAD!
WOOF!
JON, HE'S TRYING TO TELL US SOMETHING.
IT'S THE BALL OVER THERE. OF COURSE. WE NEED TO GO OVER THERE!
OKAY!

UM... WHY?
I THOUGHT YOU GOT IT THAT TIME TOO...
NOT THAT TIME, NO.
SIGH THAT BALL OF ENERGY MUST BE THE SOURCE OF THE TEMPORAL DISRUPTIONS. THE ENTITY MUST BE HIDING IN THERE!
AHA! OF COURSE! IT ONLY MAKES SENSE. EVERYONE TO THE YELLOW BALL!

PAW
ARG!!!
WHAT'S HE DOING HERE?!
JON, WE'LL HANDLE THIS. KEEP RUNNING!!!
BUT, I...
RUN!!!

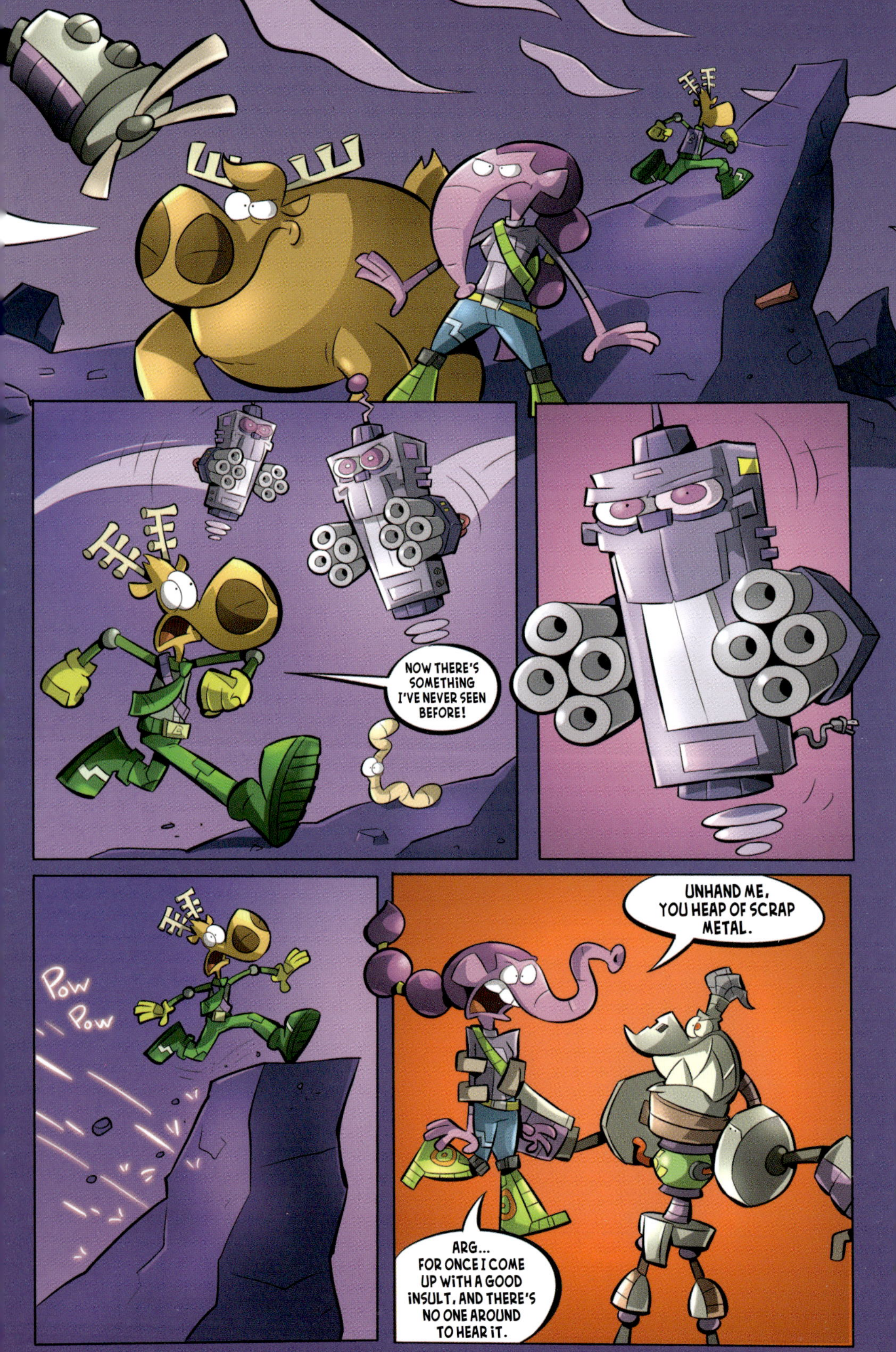
NOW THERE'S SOMETHING I'VE NEVER SEEN BEFORE!
POW POW
UNHAND ME, YOU HEAP OF SCRAP METAL.
ARG... FOR ONCE I COME UP WITH A GOOD INSULT, AND THERE'S NO ONE AROUND TO HEAR IT.

IT'S TOO FAR!!
OH YA, I ALMOST FORGOT!
CLICK
THANKS, HENRY!

JON!!!
BLOP

HELLO, LITTLE GUY!

AH!
HOW DID YOU GET IN HERE?
WELL... WITH A HAND GLIDER. IT WASN'T TOO HARD.

PLEASE DON'T HURT ME...
HUH? I'M NOT HERE TO HURT YOU! I JUST WANT TO TALK A LITTLE.

OH, OKAY.
COME SIT DOWN.

WHAT IS THIS PLACE?
YOUR WORLD SCARED ME. NO MATTER WHERE I WENT, EVERYONE THOUGHT I MEANT THEM HARM. SO I CREATED A LITTLE SHELTER OUTSIDE TIME.
ARE YOU SERIOUS? THERE'S NO TIME IN HERE?
HA HA.
THAT'S FUNNY.
THIS IS THE SECOND TIME THAT SUPERIOR BEINGS HAVE STOPPED TIME AROUND ME.
... REALLY? SO IT'S NOT VERY ORIGINAL THEN.
LISTEN, I SWEAR NO ONE WANTS TO HURT YOU. WE'RE JUST A LITTLE JUMPY IN OUR WORLD.
WELL, YOU DO LOOK NICE.
AND WHAT DO YOU PLAN TO DO SHUT AWAY IN HERE?
I'M WAITING FOR MY PARENTS TO COME GET ME. THEY SHOULDN'T BE LONG...
HOW ARE THEY GOING TO COME GET YOU IF YOU'VE STOPPED TIME?
OH... I HADN'T THOUGHT OF THAT!

LISTEN, I CAN THINK OF A MUCH BETTER WAY TO HELP YOU.
I KNOW SOMEONE, A SCIENTIST. HE COULD HELP YOU GET BACK TO YOUR WORLD.

REALLY?
REALLY! HIS NAME IS HENRY. HE'S REALLY COOL. YOU SHOULD HAVE SEEN HIS HALLOWEEN COSTUME THIS YEAR...
HE SHOULD HAVE WON.

OH OKAY! A ZOMBIE WORM! IT'S IRONIC BECAUSE WORMS EAT ZOMBIES. I JUST DIDN'T GET IT. I KNOW WHY HE WON IN THE END!
HUH?

SO, YES! ALL YOU HAVE TO DO IS RESTORE THE TIME LINE AND GET IN THIS BALL. I SWEAR WE'LL GET YOU HOME AS QUICK AS WE CAN!
OKAY! I THINK I CAN TRUST YOU. THERE'S A LOT OF LIGHT INSIDE YOU. I CAN SEE IT.
UM, I'LL TAKE THAT AS A COMPLIMENT!

OH! ONE LAST THING BEFORE YOU RESTORE ORDER... COULD YOU...
YES, OF COURSE. BUT YOU COULD HAVE ASKED ME OUT LOUD.
SO HOW DO I GET IN THERE?
IT MUST BE LIKE IN POKÉMON.
GOTTA CATCH 'EM ALL!
OUCH.

ZOOOOOOOOOOO
BOUM

EARLIER IN TIME... (YES, THAT'S RIGHT. REMEMBER, WE'RE BACK AT THIS SCENE FROM THE BEGINNING, SO, IT'S EARLIER... IN THE FUTURE. OH, WELL, FIGURE IT OUT FOR YOURSELVES...)

SO... WE CAN GO ON?
I THINK SO.

JON! SO HOW DID THE TRIP GO?
GREAT. THE ENTITY IS IN HERE.
HEY, GET YOUR HANDS OFF IT! IT'S OURS!

GRRR, SURE SURE... BUT HEY! WHERE IS MY DAUGHTER? YOU HAD ORDERS TO BRING HER BACK HERE!!!

YOUR DAUGHTER? OH! THE ONE YOU WANTED TO THROW IN JAIL? LIKE YOU DID TO ME?
WHAT?
HELLO.
MAPLE... DEAR DAUGHTER, HOW ARE YOU? HOW DID...
JON ASKED THE ENTITY TO BRING ME HOME A DAY BEFORE HIM. EVERYONE HERE ALREADY KNOWS ME AND KNOWS MY STORY.
TIME TRAVEL IS GREAT.

SO I HAD A CHANCE TO HAVE A LONG TALK WITH YOUR DAUGHTER, AND SHE IS THE IDEAL CANDIDATE FOR OUR ORGANIZATION.

SO SHE'S GOING TO INTERN IN ONE OF OUR BUILDINGS AND COULD QUALIFY TO BECOME AN AGENT IN SIX MONTHS.

YOU CAN'T...

SORRY, DAD. I'M OUT OF YOUR COMPANY FOR GOOD NOW. YOU CAN'T LOCK ME AWAY ANYMORE.

NO...

NO!!!! ARG!!!

HEY, MY CENTREPIECE!

DO YOU REALIZE WHO YOU'RE ATTACKING?! I'M THE MOST POWERFUL BEING ON EARTH! I'M GOING TO TAKE THIS BUILDING APART PIECE BY PIECE!
YOU AND WHAT ARMY?

THAT ONE...
OH.

I HAVE TO ASK YOU TO LEAVE. YOU ARE NO LONGER WELCOME HERE.
... YOUR SO-CALLED "POWER" WILL COME CRASHING DOWN ON YOUR HEAD ONE OF THESE DAYS. AND IF THE WORLD ENDS IN RUINS...

IT WILL PROBABLY BE YOUR FAULT.

THANK YOU FOR YOUR COMMENTS. WE WILL GIVE THEM DUE CONSIDERATION. GOOD EVENING.
BIP
DZZZZ
WHAT? WHAT THE...
!
HEY, MR. PRESIDENT. YOU'RE NAKED!
ARGGGRRRR...
YES!!!
WE'RE NUMBER ONE!

I'M PROUD OF YOU, SON! YOU REPAIRED THE TIME LINE ALL ON YOUR OWN! EVEN BATMAN COULDN'T DO THAT.
OH, UM... NO, IT'S TRUE. HE DID. BUT YOU'RE COOL ANYWAY!

IT'S AN HONOUR TO BE PART OF YOUR ORGANIZATION, MA'AM.
IT'S NOT MINE NOW. IT'S YOURS TOO.

HEE HEE!

JON! DO YOU REALIZE? WE'RE GOING TO SEE EACH OTHER PRACTICALLY EVERY DAY.
THAT'S GREAT!

IT MIGHT BE AN OPPORTUNITY TO... TAKE OUR RELATIONSHIP... A LITTLE FURTHER...
HMM?

SO, WOULD YOU LIKE US TO BE... MORE THAN JUST FRIENDS?
NO!
... NOT REALLY!
... WHAT? YOU'RE NOT INTERESTED?
SO LONG, EVERYBODY. UNTIL MY NEXT ADVENTURE!!
!!! ...

ALEX A.

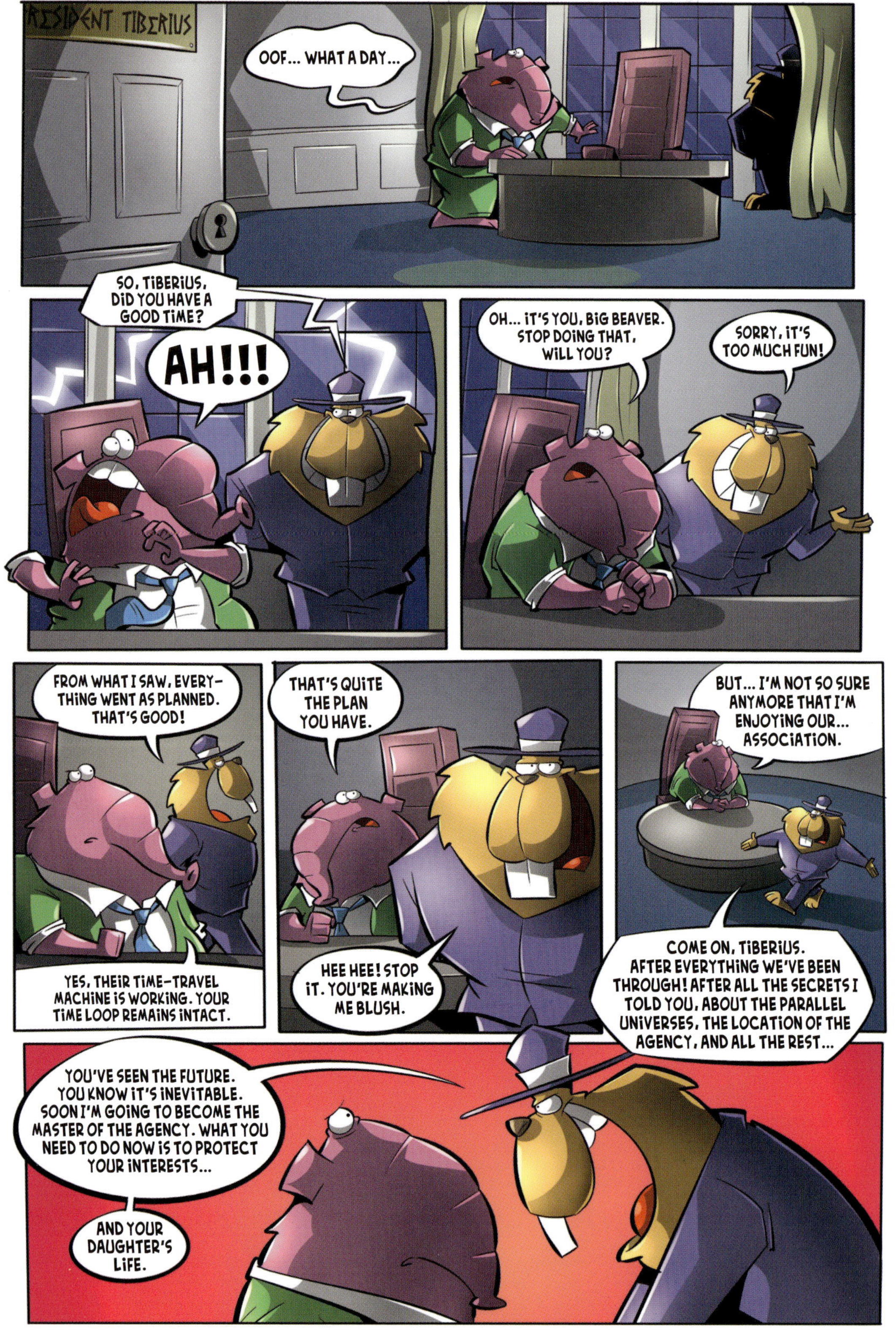
RESIDENT TIBERIUS
OOF... WHAT A DAY...
SO, TIBERIUS, DID YOU HAVE A GOOD TIME?
AH!!!
OH... IT'S YOU, BIG BEAVER. STOP DOING THAT, WILL YOU?
SORRY, IT'S TOO MUCH FUN!
FROM WHAT I SAW, EVERY-THING WENT AS PLANNED. THAT'S GOOD!
YES, THEIR TIME-TRAVEL MACHINE IS WORKING. YOUR TIME LOOP REMAINS INTACT.
THAT'S QUITE THE PLAN YOU HAVE.
HEE HEE! STOP IT. YOU'RE MAKING ME BLUSH.
BUT... I'M NOT SO SURE ANYMORE THAT I'M ENJOYING OUR... ASSOCIATION.
COME ON, TIBERIUS. AFTER EVERYTHING WE'VE BEEN THROUGH! AFTER ALL THE SECRETS I TOLD YOU, ABOUT THE PARALLEL UNIVERSES, THE LOCATION OF THE AGENCY, AND ALL THE REST...
YOU'VE SEEN THE FUTURE. YOU KNOW IT'S INEVITABLE. SOON I'M GOING TO BECOME THE MASTER OF THE AGENCY. WHAT YOU NEED TO DO NOW IS TO PROTECT YOUR INTERESTS...
AND YOUR DAUGHTER'S LIFE.

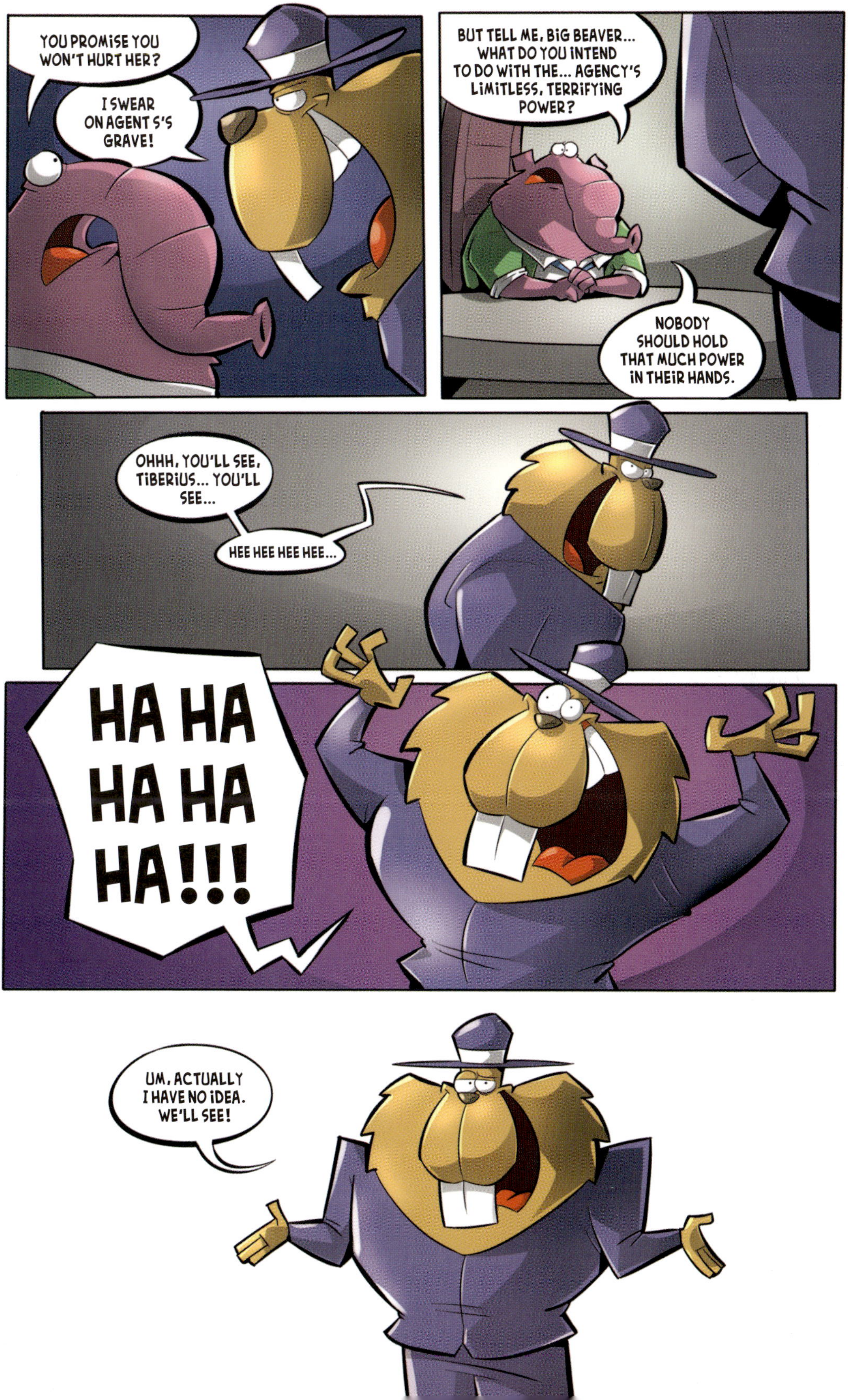

OHHH, YOU'LL SEE, TIBERIUS... YOU'LL SEE...

HEE HEE HEE HEE...

HA HA HA HA HA!!!

FIND OUT MORE ABOUT SUPER AGENT JON LE BON AT ALEX-COMICS.COM!

A GRAPHIC NOVEL SERIES THAT'S FUNNY, OFFBEAT AND BRILLIANT!

THE BRAIN OF THE APOCALYPSE

FORMULA V

OPERATION SHORTHAND

THE PROPHECY OF FOUR

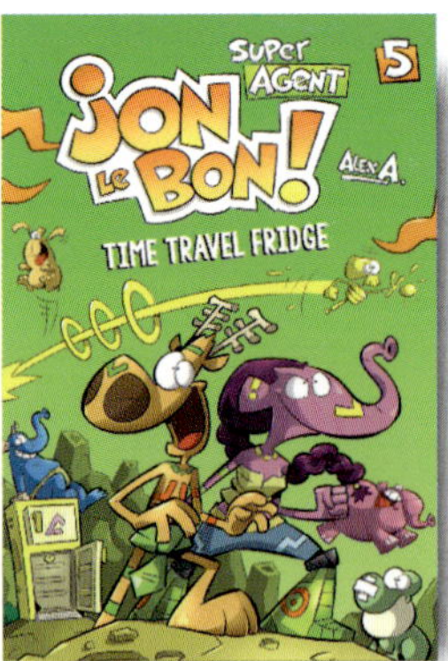

TIME TRAVEL FRIDGE

A SHEEP IN THE HEAD

COMING IN 2017